The Shadow Economy

The Shadow Economy

FRIEDRICH SCHNEIDER &
COLIN C. WILLIAMS

The Institute of Economic Affairs

First published in Great Britain in 2013 by
The Institute of Economic Affairs
2 Lord North Street
Westminster
London SW1P 3LB
in association with Profile Books Ltd

The mission of the Institute of Economic Affairs is to improve public
understanding of the fundamental institutions of a free society, with particular
reference to the role of markets in solving economic and social problems.

A CIP catalogue record for this book is available from the British Library.

ISBN 978 0 255 36674 8
eISBN 978 0 255 36688 5

Many IEA publications are translated into languages other than English or
are reprinted. Permission to translate or to reprint should be sought from the
Director General at the address above.

Typeset in Stone by MacGuru Ltd
info@macguru.org.uk

Printed and bound in Britain by Hobbs the Printers

CONTENTS

THE AUTHORS

Since 1986 Friedrich Schneider has been Professor of Economics at the Johannes Kepler University of Linz, Austria. He obtained his PhD in Economics from the University of Konstanz in 1976 and has held numerous visiting and honorary positions at a number of universities. He was the European editor of *Public Choice* from 1991 to 2004 and he has published extensively in leading economics journals, including the *Quarterly Journal of Economics*, the *American Economic Review*, the *Economic Journal* and *Kyklos*. He has published 67 books, 196 articles in scientific journals and 171 articles in edited volumes.

Colin C. Williams is Professor of Public Policy and Director of the Inter-disciplinary Centre of the Social Sciences (ICOSS) at the University of Sheffield. His recent books include *The Role of the Informal Sector in Post-Soviet Economies* (Routledge, 2013), *Informal Work in Developed Nations* (Routledge, 2010), *Rethinking the Future of Work: Directions and Visions* (Palgrave Macmillan, 2007), *The Hidden Enterprise Culture* (Edward Elgar, 2006) and *Cash-in-Hand Work* (Palgrave Macmillan, 2004).

FOREWORD

To some people, the shadow economy is a great example of free economic activity at work. It is entirely unregulated except by the participants themselves; no tax is paid on shadow economic activity; and it may be possible to pursue activities in the shadow economy which are prohibited by law unjustly. Indeed, the smugglers of Sussex are still commemorated by the uniforms worn by members of bonfire societies on Guy Fawkes Night and they were, indeed, known as 'free traders'.

At the very least, it is certainly true that, in a world in which developed country governments are spending and borrowing more and more, the possibilities for shadow economic activity place a restraint upon governments. One of the reasons for the 'Laffer curve' effect, whereby tax revenues can start to fall as tax rates are increased, is the movement of economic activity out of the taxed economy and into the shadow economy.

A different perspective can be taken, however. Firstly, shadow economy activity can be marred by gang violence and coercion with little legal redress for its victims – this was certainly true of seventeenth- and eighteenth-century smuggling. Secondly, operating in the shadow economy is a serious impediment to the expansion of businesses. Obtaining insurance, formalising employment relationships and advertising can all be difficult when a business is not legally registered. Thirdly, the existence of a large shadow economy means that tax rates are higher for those in the legal economy.

Whichever way one looks at it, the shadow economy should be of interest to those studying the operation of markets. The argument for free-market economists being interested in the shadow economy grows stronger when the causes of its growth are examined. As this monograph – written by two of the world's leading figures in this area – shows, the level of tax is one of the major drivers of shadow economic activity. If governments keep tax rates low, the shadow economy is likely to be smaller. Furthermore, if tax rates are low and the shadow economy smaller, then it is more likely that citizens will think that the tax system is 'fair'. This, in turn, raises 'tax morale' and puts further downward pressure on the shadow economy.

It is an indictment of modern government that the shadow economy is so large. A shadow economy equal to 9–12 per cent of total economic activity is not untypical for Anglo-Saxon countries, and levels of 20–30 per cent are common in southern Europe. Not only could tax rates be lower if the shadow economy were smaller but, if the size of the state were smaller, the shadow economy would be smaller.

As well as looking at the size and causes of the shadow economy, the authors examine detailed evidence about participation in the shadow economy. These issues are also important. If participants in the shadow economy are also claiming welfare benefits for unemployment the focus when dealing with the shadow economy should, perhaps, be on the welfare system. On the other hand, if shadow work is mainly being undertaken in the spare time of people who are in the regular labour market, strategies should be different.

Indeed, the authors do examine strategies for reducing shadow economic activity. Policy proposals include making it easier for businesses to legally register their activity and also tax amnesties. In many cases, these policies have a proven record of success in other countries. To this policy armoury should be added a wider policy agenda of deregulation and lower taxation which, according to the earlier parts of the study, are policies that are likely to be conducive to a smaller shadow economy.

Understanding the shadow economy is important for understanding the impact that the growing size of government has on our lives. This area is a notoriously difficult one to research – after all, the activity is illegal and so will not be officially recorded. The authors of this monograph have done a marvellous job in compiling and analysing this information, and the IEA is delighted to bring it to a wider audience through our Hobart Paper series.

The views expressed in this monograph are, as in all IEA publications, those of the authors and not those of the Institute (which has no corporate view), its managing trustees, Academic Advisory Council members or senior staff. With some exceptions, such as with the publication of lectures, all IEA monographs are blind peer-reviewed by at least two academics or researchers who are experts in the field.

PHILIP BOOTH

Editorial and Programme Director,
Institute of Economic Affairs,
Professor of Insurance and Risk Management,
Cass Business School, City University, London
March 2013

SUMMARY

- Measurement of the shadow economy is notoriously difficult as it requires estimation of economic activity that is deliberately hidden from official transactions. Surveys typically understate the size of the shadow economy but econometric techniques can now be used to obtain a much better understanding of its size.
- The shadow economy constitutes approximately 10 per cent of GDP in the UK; about 14 per cent in Nordic countries and about 20–30 per cent in many southern European countries.
- The main drivers of the shadow economy are (in order): tax and social security burdens, tax morale, the quality of state institutions and labour market regulation. A reduction in the tax burden is therefore likely to lead to a reduction in the size of the shadow economy. Indeed, a virtuous circle can be created of lower tax rates, less shadow work, higher tax morale, a higher tax take and the opportunity for lower rates. Of course, a vicious circle in the other direction can also be created.
- Given this relationship, the high level of non-wage costs (averaging 39 per cent of total labour costs) and the penalty on individuals who move from earning one third to two thirds of the median wage (averaging 58 per cent of the

increase in earnings for a one-earner couple) in the European Union should be a matter of real concern. The latter figure is 79 per cent in the UK and thus low-paid UK workers have a huge incentive to supplement their incomes in the shadow economy.

- The number of participants in the shadow economy is very large. Although up-to-date figures are not available, at the end of the twentieth century up to 30 million people performed shadow work in the EU and up to 48 million in the OECD. Reliable detailed studies are not available for many countries. In Denmark, however, the latest studies suggest that about half the population purchases shadow work. In some sectors – such as construction – about half the workforce is working in the shadow economy, often in addition to formal employment. Only a very small proportion of shadow economy workers can be accounted for by illegal immigrants in most countries.

- In western Europe, shadow work is relatively prevalent among the unemployed and the formally employed. Other non-employed (for example, the retired, homemakers and students) do relatively less shadow work. This has implications for policy in terms of the importance of social security systems that reduce the opportunities for shadow work among the unemployed and the importance of tax systems that do not discourage the declaring of extra income.

- Policies focused on deterrence are not likely to be especially successful when tackling the shadow economy. The shadow economy is pervasive and made up of a huge number of small and highly dispersed transactions. We should also be wary about trying to stamp out the shadow economy as we may stamp out the entrepreneurship and business formation that goes with it.

- There are, however, huge potential benefits from allowing the self-employed and small businesses to formalise their arrangements. Businesses cannot flourish if they remain in the shadow economy. They might be reluctant to formalise, however, if it involves admitting to past indiscretions. Worthwhile policies include: reducing business compliance regulation; amnesties; providing limited tax shelters for small-scale informal activity such as the provision of interest-bearing loans to relatives and friends; and allowing businesses to formalise using simple 'off the shelf' models. Such policies have been successful in other countries – and to a limited extent in the UK – with high benefit-to-cost ratios.

- Given that the shadow economy constitutes a high proportion of national income, and varies between less than 8 per cent of national income and over 30 per cent of national income in OECD countries, official national income statistics can often be misleading. Comparisons are made even more difficult because some countries adjust figures for the shadow economy (for example, Italy) and others do not.

- In less developed countries, the informal sector constitutes typically between 25 and 40 per cent of national income and represents up to 70 per cent of non-agricultural employment. In such countries, informal activity often arises because of the inadequacies of legal systems when it comes to formalising business registration.

TABLES AND FIGURES

1 INTRODUCTION

Reducing tax evasion, the shadow economy and informal employment has been an important policy goal in OECD countries during recent decades. The shadow economy is notoriously difficult to measure, however. Given the difficulties in measuring the shadow economy, statistical work on its causes and how to deal with it is especially problematic. Nevertheless, data is available that can help us explore these issues. But, why is it important to try to know more about the shadow economy?

Shadow economic activity is problematic for several reasons. One of the purposes of government is to provide the legal framework within which economic activity takes place; and societies with good institutions prosper. But when it comes to shadow work those legal institutions are bypassed: contracts can often be unenforceable; economic relationships can become marred by violence; and it can become very difficult for businesses to expand because they then come to the attention of the authorities. A large shadow economy also means that tax rates are higher for those working in the formal economy. Furthermore, as is shown in this monograph, there is a relationship between the size of the tax burden and the size of the shadow economy.

As such, understanding the shadow economy has important policy implications. Firstly, there is a need to create an environment in which economic activity can easily be formalised – where there are as few regulatory impediments to formalisation as possible. Secondly, at a broader level, the shadow economy provides a further argument for the need to educate people about the purpose of taxation so as to improve tax morality and hence compliance. Thirdly, there is a need to ensure that the tax system itself is not of a scale and design such that it encourages shadow economic activity.

When it comes to measuring the shadow economy there are a number of challenges. Several methods are used in practice and they tend to give different results. Survey measures, for example, tend to understate the size of the shadow economy because, even in the most carefully controlled of circumstances, people do not like to admit to shadow work – and sometimes they persuade themselves that they are not really undertaking shadow work. Newer statistical techniques have been developed that provide more credible evidence about the size of the shadow economy, and the measures derived from these techniques can then be calibrated using variables, such as the amount of cash in an economy, which are known to be related to the extent of shadow economic activity.

The results may surprise those not familiar with the literature. A shadow economy of around 9–12 per cent of total economic activity is not untypical for Anglo-Saxon countries, and levels of 20–30 per cent are common in southern Europe. The size of the shadow economy has not varied dramatically over the last decade or so; if anything it has decreased slightly, at least until the outbreak of the euro crisis. The number of participants in the shadow economy is also very large: perhaps 30 million people in the EU alone.

Because of the relationship between the size of the shadow

economy and the level of taxation, there is a danger of a vicious circle being created in certain circumstances. If the tax burden rises, we might get more shadow work, lower tax receipts, and then yet higher tax rates as the government tries to raise more revenue from a smaller tax base. This may cause yet further increases in the shadow economy, and so on. Of course, this vicious circle can be reversed and turned virtuous if the right policies are pursued. A further factor influencing the size of the shadow economy is 'tax morale'. If people think that the tax system is becoming less fair and that their neighbours are dodging tax, they are more likely to work in the shadow economy too. This can also contribute to the vicious and virtuous circle effects.

As such, successful policies to tackle the shadow economy are of some significance. When it comes to trying to reduce its size, it is interesting to note that policies focused on deterrence do not tend to be especially successful. The shadow economy is pervasive and made up of a huge number of small and highly dispersed transactions. Furthermore, if we rely on deterrence to reduce the shadow economy we may stamp out the entrepreneurship and business formation that go with it. As we show later in this monograph, there are huge potential benefits from taking a different approach and making it easier to enable the self-employed and small businesses to formalise their arrangements. This can include the use of amnesties that forgive previous indiscretions. Such policies have been successful in various countries with high benefit-to-cost ratios.

There is also a very large shadow economy in many less developed countries. Here we use the less 'loaded' term 'informal economy' to describe this activity because its characteristics are different from the shadow economy in the West. The informal sector in poorer countries is typically between 25 and 40 per cent of national income and can represent up to 70 per cent of non-agricultural employment. In such countries, informal activity often arises because of the inadequacies of legal systems when it comes to formalising business registration rather than as a result of deliberate evasion activity. Nevertheless, the problems that informality can bring are enormous: it can be a serious constraint on business growth; and the lack of enforceability of business and employment contracts in a country makes prosperity much harder to achieve. Rather than proposing solutions to these specific problems in this monograph, we point the reader to the literature in development economics, such as that by De Soto (2000).

The remainder of the monograph is organised as follows: Chapter 2 discusses the definition of the shadow economy and also its measurement. We then move on to examine the main causes of shadow economic activity before presenting the latest research on the size of the shadow economy worldwide. There is then a more detailed analysis of the shadow economy labour market and the relationship between the size of the shadow economy and unemployment. Finally, we consider various ways in which the shadow economy can be reduced. The appendices examine how shadow economic activity is taken into account in official national income statistics and provide further information on the size of the shadow economy country by country.

2 HOW TO MEASURE THE SHADOW ECONOMY

Defining the shadow economy

Most authors trying to measure the shadow economy still face the difficulty of a precise definition.[1] According to one commonly used definition it comprises all currently unregistered economic activities that would contribute to the officially calculated gross national product if the activities were recorded.[2] P. Smith (1994: 18) defines the shadow economy as 'market-based production of goods and services, whether legal or illegal, that escapes detection in the official estimates of GDP'. Put differently, one of the broadest definitions is: 'those economic activities and the income derived from them that circumvent or otherwise avoid

---

1   This monograph focuses on the size and development of the shadow economy for individual countries and not for regions. Recently first studies have been undertaken to measure the size of the shadow economy as well as the 'grey' or 'shadow' labour force for urban regions or states (e.g. California). See, e.g., Marcelli et al. (1999), Marcelli (2004), Chen (2004), Williams and Windebank (1998, 2001a, 2001b), Flaming et al. (2005), Alderslade et al. (2006), Brück et al. (2006). Herwartz et al. (2009) and Tafenau et al. (2010) estimate the size of the shadow economy of 234 EU-NUTS regions for the year 2004, for the first time demonstrating a considerable regional variation in the size of the shadow economy.
2   This definition is used, for example, by Feige (1989, 1994), Schneider (1994a, 2003, 2005) and Frey and Pommerehne (1984). Do-it-yourself activities are not included. For estimates of the shadow economy and do-it-yourself activities for Germany, see Bühn et al. (2009) or Karmann (1986, 1990).

government regulation, taxation or observation'.[3] As these definitions still leave room for interpretation, Table 1 provides examples of a reasonable consensus definition of the underground (or shadow) economy according to its broadest definition.

Table 1 **Taxonomy of types of underground economic activities**

Type of activity	Monetary transactions		Non-monetary transactions	
ILLEGAL ACTIVITIES	Trade in stolen goods; drug dealing and manufacturing; prostitution; gambling; smuggling; fraud; human trafficking, drug trafficking and weapon trafficking.		Barter of drugs, stolen goods, smuggling, etc.; producing or growing drugs for own use; theft.	
	Tax evasion	Tax avoidance	Tax evasion	Tax avoidance
LEGAL ACTIVITIES	Unreported income from self-employment; wages, salaries and assets from unreported work related to legal services and goods	Employee discounts; fringe benefits	Barter of legal services and goods	All do-it-yourself work and neighbour help

Source: The structure of the table is taken from Lippert and Walker (1997: 5) with additional remarks

From Table 1, it is obvious that a broad definition of the

---

3   This definition is taken from Dell'Anno (2003), Dell'Anno and Schneider (2003) and Feige (1989); see also Thomas (1999), Fleming et al. (2000) or Feld and Larsen (2005: 25).

shadow economy includes unreported income from the production of legal goods and services, either from monetary or barter transactions – and so includes all productive economic activities that would generally be taxable were they reported to the state (tax) authorities. In this monograph this narrower definition of the shadow economy is used, though it should be noted that it is a subset of a wider definition.[4] We will measure the shadow economy insofar as it includes all market-based production of legal goods and services that are deliberately concealed from public authorities for the following reasons:

- to avoid payment of income, value added or other taxes;
- to avoid payment of social security contributions;
- to avoid having to meet certain legal labour market standards, such as minimum wages, maximum working hours, safety standards, etc.; and
- to avoid complying with certain administrative obligations.

Thus, we will not deal with typically illegal underground economic activities that fit the characteristics of classic crimes such as burglary, robbery, drug dealing, etc. We also exclude the informal household economy, which consists of all household services and production. Table 2 gives examples of activities that are inside and outside the shadow economy according to this definition.

---

4   See also the excellent discussion of the definition of the shadow economy in Pedersen (2003: 13–19) and Kazemier (2005a), who use a similar definition.

Table 2 **Sample activities and the shadow economy**

Activity	Inside or outside our measure of the shadow economy	Reason if outside
Child-minding with income not declared	Inside	n/a
Selling drugs	Outside	Activity not legal
Paying builder cash, income not declared	Inside	n/a
Building work done by homeowner	Outside	Do-it-yourself activity not subject to tax or regulation
Purchase of cigarettes smuggled from EU country	Inside	n/a
Counterfeit production of an otherwise legal product such as cigarettes	Inside	n/a

This definition will therefore not capture do-it-yourself activity even if it is undertaken to avoid tax and regulation because such activity is perfectly legal. It also will not capture illegal activities such as drug smuggling, though it will capture, for example, the production and sale of alcohol on the black market.

The definition of the shadow economy plays an important role in assessing its size. By having a clear definition, a number of ambiguities and controversies can be avoided, though some important shadow economic activity will be omitted. The extent of the activities we omit, such as non-marketed household work, may well be affected by the same factors as affect the size of the shadow economy as defined here (for example, the level of taxes), but they raise different issues as well as measurement problems.

The economic activities we focus on contribute to the country's value added even though they are not captured in the national accounts.[5] From the economic and social perspective, soft forms of illicit employment and their contribution to aggregate value added can be assessed rather positively.

Measuring the shadow economy[6]

Although the shadow economy has been investigated for a long time, discussion regarding the 'appropriate' methodology to assess its scope has not come to an end yet.[7] Measurement is very difficult because of the very nature of shadow economic activity. In general, there are three methods of assessment of the size of the shadow economy that are used:

- Direct procedures at a micro level that aim at determining the size of the shadow economy at one particular point in time. An example is the survey method.
- Indirect procedures that make use of macroeconomic indicators in order to proxy the development of the shadow economy over time.
- Statistical models that use statistical tools to estimate the shadow economy as an 'unobserved' variable.

The most commonly used method of measurement is based on

5　Compare Chapter 6, however, where it is shown that shadow economy activities are partly captured in the official statistics in some countries.

6　Compare also Feld and Schneider (2010) and Schneider (2011).

7　For the strengths and weaknesses of the various methods, see Bhattacharyya (1999), Breusch (2005a, 2005b), Dell'Anno and Schneider (2009), Dixon (1999), Feige (1989), Feld and Larsen (2005), Feld and Schneider (2010), Giles (1999a, 1999b, 1999c), Schneider (1986, 2001, 2003, 2005, 2006, 2011), Schneider and Enste (2000a, 2000b, 2002, 2006), Tanzi (1999), Thomas (1992, 1999).

a combination of the multiple indicator multiple cause (MIMIC) procedure and on the currency demand method, or, alternatively, the use of only the currency demand method.[8]

The MIMIC procedure assumes that the shadow economy remains an unobserved phenomenon (a latent variable) which can be estimated using quantitatively measurable causes of shadow economic activity as well as indicators of illicit activity. The causes will include variables such as the tax burden and the intensity of regulation and the indicators will include variables such as the demand for currency, official national income figures and official working hours data. The econometric models are complex and have to deal with a range of well-known challenges such as endogeneity problems. For example, the size of the tax burden might 'cause' an increase in the size of the shadow economy. At the same time, an increase in the size of the shadow economy might make it more difficult for the government to raise taxes so it responds by raising tax rates and therefore the tax burden on the level of official national income. These problems can be overcome and are discussed in later chapters.

A disadvantage of the MIMIC procedure is that it produces only relative estimates of the size and development of the shadow economy. Thus, the currency demand method[9] is used to calibrate

---

8   These methods are presented in detail in Schneider (1994a, 1994b, 1994c, 2005, 2011), Feld and Schneider (2010) and Schneider and Enste (2000b, 2002, 2006). Furthermore, these studies discuss advantages and disadvantages of the MIMIC and the money demand methods as well as other estimation methods for assessing the size of illicit employment; for a detailed discussion see also Feld and Larsen (2005).

9   This indirect approach is based on the assumption that cash is used to make transactions within the shadow economy. By using this method one econometrically estimates a currency demand function including independent variables such as tax burden, regulation, etc., which 'drive' the shadow economy. This

the relative value into absolute value estimates (for example, as a percentage of national income) by using two or three absolute values (as a percentage of GDP) of the size of the shadow economy.

In addition, the size of the shadow economy is estimated by using survey methods (see, for example, Feld and Larsen, 2005, 2008, 2009). Such direct procedures are likely to underestimate the shadow economy because people are likely to under-declare in surveys the activity that they are trying to hide from the authorities. In order to minimise the number of respondents dishonestly replying or totally declining answers to the sensitive questions, structured interviews are undertaken (usually face to face) in which the respondents slowly become accustomed to the main purpose of the survey. In some respects, this is rather like the contingent valuation method (CVM) in environmental economics (Kopp et al. 1997). The first part of the questionnaire aims at shaping respondents' perception of the issue at hand. The second part asks questions about respondents' activities in the shadow economy. The third part contains the usual socio-demographic questions. Nevertheless, as will be seen below, the results of shadow economy estimates from the survey method are clearly (low) outliers compared with the other approaches.

Survey results can also be inconsistent internationally. In addition to the studies by Merz and Wolff (1993), Feld and Larsen (2005, 2008, 2009), Haigner et al. (2011) and Enste and

---

equation is used to make simulations of the amount of money that would be necessary to generate official GDP. This amount is then compared with the actual money demand and the difference is treated as an indicator of the development of the shadow economy. On this basis the calculated difference is multiplied by the velocity of money of the official economy and one gets a value added figure for the shadow economy.

Schneider (2006) for Germany, the survey method has been applied in the Nordic countries and Great Britain (Isachsen and Strøm, 1985; Pedersen, 2003) as well as in the Netherlands (Van Eck and Kazemier, 1988; Kazemier, 2006). While the questionnaires underlying these studies are broadly comparable in design, however, recent attempts by the European Union to provide survey results for all member states have run into difficulties of comparability (Renooy et al., 2004; European Commission, 2007). The wording of the questionnaires becomes more and more cumbersome depending on the culture of different countries with respect to the underground economy.

These two sets of approaches are the approaches that are most broadly used in the literature. Although each has its drawbacks and although biases in the estimates of the shadow economy almost certainly prevail, no better data are currently available. There is no exact measure of the size of the shadow economy – after all, the whole point is that we are trying to measure economic activity that is not recorded. Each method has its strengths and weaknesses (shown in detail in Schneider and Enste, 2000b). Estimates of the size of the shadow economy by the MIMIC method are generally thought to have a margin of error of +/–15 per cent (that is, there is a probability of 95 per cent that the true value of the shadow economy is between 8.5 per cent and 11.5 per cent of national income if the estimated value is 10 per cent). The estimates using the MIMIC and currency demand approaches are generally regarded as being towards the upper bound of the true value of the shadow economy, though it should be noted that we have defined the shadow economy relatively narrowly. Survey estimates certainly form lower-bound estimates for the reasons discussed above.

There are other ways of investigating the shadow economy. In tax compliance research, the most interesting data stem from tax audits by the US Internal Revenue Service (IRS). In the Taxpayer Compliance Measurement Program (TCMP), actual compliance behaviour of taxpayers is observed and is used for empirical analysis (see Andreoni et al., 1998). The approach of the IRS is broader in a certain sense as tax evasion from all sources of income is considered while the other methods of estimating the shadow economy mainly measure tax evasion from labour income. Even the data obtained from the TCMP is biased, however, because the tax non-compliance actually detected may well only be the tip of the iceberg. Nevertheless, the imperfect data in this area can still provide insights into the size, the development and the determinants of the shadow economy and of the shadow economy labour force.

3 THE MAIN DRIVERS OF THE SHADOW ECONOMY

It is important to understand the main determinants of the shadow economy both because it informs policy in relation to dealing with the problem and also because understanding the determinants of the shadow economy is important for the MIMIC method of estimation that is generally used below. The main causes relate to the level of taxes, regulation, public institutions and deterrence.

Relationships between causes of the shadow economy

A useful starting point for a theoretical discussion of tax non-compliance is the paper by Allingham and Sandmo (1972) on income tax evasion. While the shadow economy and tax evasion are not congruent, activities in the shadow economy in most cases imply the evasion of direct or indirect taxes so that the factors affecting tax evasion will most certainly also affect the shadow economy. According to Allingham and Sandmo, tax compliance depends on its expected costs and benefits. The benefits of tax non-compliance result from the individual marginal tax rate that is avoided and the true individual income, including non-declared income. When we look at the shadow economy and its relationship with individual marginal tax rates, we calculate the overall marginal tax burden from indirect and direct taxes, including social security contributions. The individual income generated in the shadow economy is usually categorised as labour income though sometimes it may be capital income. The expected costs of non-compliance derive from deterrence measures pursued by the state which determine the probability of detection and also the fines individuals face when they are caught. As individual morality also plays a role in compliance, additional costs could pertain beyond pure punishment by the tax administration in the form of psychic costs such as shame or regret. There may also be additional costs arising from, for example, a loss of reputation that may damage a business.

Kanniainen et al. (2004) incorporate many of these insights in their model of the shadow economy by also considering labour supply decisions. They hypothesise that higher taxes unambiguously increase the shadow economy, while the effect of public goods financed by those taxes on the shadow economy depends on the ability to access public goods. Morality is also included in this analysis. The costs for individual non-compliers resulting from moral norms, however, appear to be mainly captured by state punishment, although self-esteem does play a role.

A shortcoming of these analyses is the possible endogeneity of tax morale and good governance. Tax morale is the phenomenon by which there is a greater tendency to declare income and pay taxes if taxpayers believe that the tax system is broadly fair, that others are paying their fair share, and so on. It is highly likely, of course, that good governance will increase tax morale. It is also possible that strong tax morale will create the conditions in which good governance is more likely to thrive. It might therefore be difficult to separate cause from effect.

Tax compliance can be thought of as the result of a

complicated interaction between tax morale and deterrence measures (see Feld and Frey, 2007). It must be clear to taxpayers what the rules of the game are, and deterrence measures serve as signals of the tax morale a society wants to elicit (Posner, 2000a, 2000b). At the same time, however, deterrence could also crowd out the intrinsic motivation to pay taxes. Moreover, tax morale is not only increased if taxpayers perceive the public goods received in exchange for their tax payments worth the cost of paying taxes; it also increases if political decisions regarding public activities are perceived to follow fair procedures and if the treatment of taxpayers by the tax authorities is perceived to be friendly and fair. As such, tax morale is certainly not exogenously given, but is influenced by deterrence, the quality of state institutions and the constitutional differences among states.

Already, we have a rich set of variables that might influence the size of the shadow economy. This is only the starting point, however. As labour supply decisions are involved, labour and product market regulations determine the extent of shadow economic behaviour. This is important when looking at approaches to reduce the size of the shadow economy. Differentiated policies on several levels may be helpful.

Deterrence and the shadow economy[1]

Theory suggests an unambiguous relationship between deterrence and the size of the shadow economy. There is surprisingly little that is known about the effects of deterrence in practice, however. In their survey on tax compliance, Andreoni et al. (1998) report

---

1   This part is taken from Feld and Schneider (2010: 115–16).

that deterrence matters for tax evasion but that the reported effects are rather small. Blackwell (2009) finds strong deterrence effects from fines and audits in experimental tax evasion. Regarding the shadow economy, however, there is little evidence.

This is due to the fact that consistent data on the legal background and the frequency of audits are not available on an international basis. The data would be difficult to collect even for individual OECD member countries and are even more difficult to collect more widely. A recent study by Feld et al. (2007) demonstrates the difficulties in collecting the data in Germany. The legal background is quite complicated with different fines and punishment according to the severity of the offence, the level of the true income of the non-complier and also directives given to courts in different *Länder*. Moreover, the tax authorities at the state level do not reveal how intensively auditing is taking place.

With the available data on fines and audits, Feld et al. (ibid.) have conducted a time series analysis using the estimates of the shadow economy obtained using the MIMIC approach. This is a very detailed investigation with a rich data set. According to the authors' results, deterrence does not have a consistent effect on the German shadow economy. Conducting Granger causality tests, the direction of causation (in the sense of precedence) is ambiguous, leaving open the possibility that the causality runs from a falling size of the shadow economy to a higher level of deterrence rather than deterrence reducing the shadow economy.

A different approach is taken by Feld and Larsen (2005, 2008, 2009), who use individual survey data for Germany. First, replicating Pedersen (2003), who reports a negative impact of the subjectively perceived risk of detection by state audits on the probability of working in the shadow economy for the year 2001, they extend that work by adding subjectively perceived measures of fines and punishment. The levels of fines and punishment do not exert a negative influence on the shadow economy in any of the annual waves of surveys, nor in the pooled regressions for the years 2004–07 (about eight thousand observations overall). The subjectively perceived risk of detection has a robust and significant negative impact in individual years only for women. In the pooled sample for 2004–07, which minimises sampling problems, the probability of detection has a significantly negative effect on the probability of working in the shadow economy for both men and women and is robust across different specifications.[2]

Marginally significant negative effects of the perceived risk of detection of conducting undeclared work in the shadow economy for men in Denmark in 2001 have been detected by Pedersen (2003). Similar results have been obtained for men in Norway in 1998–2002 (in this case highly significant)[3] and for men and women in Sweden in 1998 (highly significant in the first case and marginally significant in the second case). No significant effect from increased detection, however, was found for Great Britain for the year 2000. Van Eck and Kazemier (1988) report a significant negative effect of a higher perceived probability of detection on participation in the hidden labour market for the Netherlands in 1982/83.

Expected fines and punishments were not included as explanatory variables in any of these studies. This is important because it is the combination of fines, other punishments and the

---

2   An earlier study by Merz and Wolff (1993) does not analyse the impact of deterrence on undeclared work.

3   The earlier study by Isachsen and Strøm (1985) for Norway also does not properly analyse the impact of deterrence on undeclared work.

risk of detection which is normally assumed to affect the shadow economy. As such, the large-scale survey study of Germany by Feld and Larsen (2005, 2009) thus appears to be the most careful analysis of deterrence effects on undeclared work to date.

Thus, overall, there would seem to be some evidence that the risk of detection may well be somewhat important – it is difficult to state the case more strongly than this. Fines and punishments seem less important than detection. The reasons for the unconvincing evidence of deterrence effects are discussed in the tax compliance literature by Andreoni et al. (1998), Kirchler (2007) and Feld and Frey (2007). One explanation is the interaction between tax morale and deterrence: if there are more draconian punishments or more intrusive methods of detection then tax morale might fall. Another is simply that taxpayers misunderstand the level of punishments and the risk of being caught evading tax. The insignificant findings for fines and punishment may also result from shortcomings in the survey design.

Tax and social security contribution burdens

In contrast to deterrence, almost all studies find that tax and social security contribution levels are among the main causes of the shadow economy.[4] Since taxes affect labour–leisure choices and increases labour supply to the shadow economy, the distortion of the overall tax burden is a major concern. The bigger the difference between the total labour cost in the official economy

---

4   See Thomas (1992), Lippert and Walker (1997), Schneider (1994a, 1994b, 1994c, 1997, 1998a, 1998b, 1999, 2000, 2003, 2005, 2009), Johnson et al. (1998a, 1998b), Tanzi (1999), Giles (1999a), Mummert and Schneider (2001), Giles and Tedds (2002) and Dell'Anno (2003).

and after-tax earnings from work, the greater is the incentive to reduce the tax wedge by working in the shadow economy. Both the levels of social security taxes and the overall tax burden are key determinants of both the existence of and changes in the size of the shadow economy.

Intensity of regulation

Increased intensity of regulations – for example, labour market regulations, trade barriers and labour restrictions for immigrants – is another important factor which reduces the freedom of choice for individuals engaged in the official economy. Intuitively, one would expect this to lead to greater shadow economic activity, and Johnson et al. (1998b) do find significant empirical evidence that this is the case. The impact is also clearly described and derived theoretically in other studies, for example in Deregulierungskommission[5] (1991) in the case of Germany.[6]

Regulation leads to a substantial increase in labour costs in the official economy. But since most of these costs can be shifted on to employees through lower wages in the official economy, such regulations provide incentives for people to work in the shadow economy, where they can be avoided. Of course, where it is illegal for migrants to work – or very difficult for them to obtain permits – it becomes highly likely that they will work in the shadow economy, especially as they may not be able to legally claim welfare benefits. Johnson et al. (1997) report empirical evidence

---

5 Deregulation Commisson.
6 The importance of regulation on the official and shadow economy has been investigated more recently by Loayza, Oviedo and Servén (2005a, 2005b). Kucera and Roncolato (2008) extensively analyse the impact of labour market regulation on the shadow economy.

supporting their model, which predicts that countries with higher regulation of their economies tend to have a larger shadow economy. They conclude that it is the enforcement of regulation which is the key factor determining the burden on firms and individuals and which drives workers into the shadow economy: regulation which is not enforced is less relevant. Friedman et al. (2000) arrive at a similar conclusion. In their study every available measure of regulation is significantly correlated with the share of the unofficial economy and the estimated sign of the relationship is unambiguous: more regulation is correlated with a larger shadow economy.

Public sector services and institutions

Better public services and institutions can reduce shadow economic activity. Furthermore, the interaction of public services with the effects of changes in tax rates can bring about dynamic effects. An increase in the shadow economy can lead to reduced government revenues which, in turn, can reduce the quality and quantity of government-provided goods and services. Ultimately, this can lead to an increase in tax rates for firms and individuals in the official sector as the government tries to raise more revenue, with the consequence of even stronger incentives to participate in the shadow economy. There is the possibility of a vicious circle developing here, with high tax rates increasing shadow economic activity, which reduces tax revenues and the quality of public services. This leads to higher tax rates, which encourage further increases in the shadow economy. Of course, a virtuous circle in the other direction can also develop if the right policies are put in place.

Johnson et al. (1998a, 1998b) present a simple model of this relationship. According to their findings, smaller shadow economies occur in countries with higher tax revenues achieved by lower tax rates, fewer laws and regulations and less bribery. Countries with a better rule of law also have smaller shadow economies. Transition countries tend to have higher levels of regulation leading to a significantly higher incidence of bribery, higher effective taxes on official activities and a large discretionary framework of regulations and consequently a higher shadow economy. Their overall conclusion is that wealthier countries of the OECD, as well as some countries in eastern Europe, find themselves in the 'good equilibrium' of a relatively low tax and regulatory burden; sizeable revenue mobilization; good rule of law and corruption control; and a (relatively) small unofficial economy. By contrast, a number of countries in Latin America and the former Soviet Union exhibit characteristics consistent with a 'bad equilibrium'. These countries have a high tax and regulatory burden on firms and a high level of discretion; the rule of law is weak; there is a high incidence of bribery; and there is a relatively high share of activities in the unofficial economy (Johnson et al., 1998a: 1).

The quality of public institutions also plays a direct role in determining the size of the shadow economy.[7] The efficient application of tax systems and regulations by government play a crucial role in the decision to conduct undeclared work, and this may be even more important than the actual burden of taxes and regulations. In particular, corruption of bureaucracy and government

---

7   See, for example, Johnson et al. (1998a, 1998b), Friedman et al. (2000), Dreher and Schneider (2009), Dreher et al. (2007, 2009), as well as Teobaldelli (2011), Teobaldelli and Schneider (2012), Schneider (2010) and Bühn and Schneider (2011).

officials seems to be associated with larger unofficial activity, while a good rule of law and secure property rights and contract enforceability increase the benefits of working in the formal sector.

Different forms of political and constitutional systems may be more or less conducive to the growth of the shadow economy. The development of the informal sector may well, at least in part, be the consequence of the failure to promote an efficient market economy operating in an appropriate framework of institutions. A federal system may have some advantages. In a federal system, competition among jurisdictions and the mobility of individuals act as constraints on politicians, who have incentives to adopt policies which are closer to a majority of voters' preferences. Efficient policies are characterised by a transparent system of taxation, with the proceeds mostly spent on productive public services. In fact, production in the formal sector benefits from a higher quality of provision of public services and is negatively affected by taxation, while the shadow economy reacts in the opposite way. Thus the ideal is low taxes that are efficiently spent. In federal systems, fiscal policy tends to be more closely aligned with a majority of voters' preferences and the size of the informal sector is lower. Not only would we expect the size of the shadow economy to be lower in federal systems than in unitary states, we would expect the use of direct democracy to be conducive to a smaller shadow economy. Teobaldelli and Schneider (2012) have found that is so and that the negative relationship between direct democracy and the size of the shadow economy is statistically significant.

Tax morale

In addition to the incentive effects discussed before, the efficiency of the public sector has an indirect effect on the size of the shadow economy because it affects tax morale. As Feld and Frey (2007) argue, tax compliance is driven by a psychological tax contract that entails rights and obligations from taxpayers and citizens on the one hand, but also from the state and its tax authorities on the other hand. Taxpayers are more inclined to pay their taxes honestly if they get valuable public services in exchange. It is important to note, however, that taxpayers may well generally be honest even in cases when they do not derive direct benefits from the public services on which their taxes are spent. In other words, taxpayers will tolerate redistributive policies if the political decisions underlying such policies follow fair procedures. Finally, the treatment of individual taxpayers by the tax authority plays a role. If taxpayers are treated like partners in a tax contract instead of subordinates in a hierarchical relationship, taxpayers will stick to the obligations of the psychological tax contract more easily. In addition to the empirical evidence on these arguments reported by Feld and Frey (ibid.), Kirchler (2007) presents a comprehensive discussion of the influence of such factors on tax compliance.

Regarding the impact of tax morale on the shadow economy, there is scarce and only recent evidence. Using data on the shadow economy obtained by the MIMIC approach, Torgler and Schneider (2009) report the most convincing evidence for a negative effect of tax morale on the shadow economy. They particularly address causality issues and establish a causal relationship from tax morale to the size of the shadow economy. This effect is also robust when additional explanatory factors and specifications are included. These findings are in line with earlier preliminary evidence by Körner et al. (2006). Using survey data, Feld and Larsen (2005, 2009) likewise report a robust negative effect of tax morale in particular and social norms more generally on the probability of respondents conducting undeclared work. Interestingly, the estimated effects of social norms on the shadow economy are quantitatively more important than the estimated deterrence effects. Van Eck and Kazemier (1988) also report a marginally significant effect of tax morale on participation in the shadow economy.

Summary of the main causes of the shadow economy

Table 3 summarises a number of empirical studies of the various factors influencing the shadow economy. The overview is based on the studies in which the size of the shadow economy is measured by the MIMIC or currency demand approach. As there is no firm evidence on the effect of deterrence using these approaches – at least with respect to the broad panel database on which this table draws – this variable is not included in the table. This is an obvious shortcoming of the studies, but one that cannot be addressed easily owing to the lack of internationally comparable data. In Table 3, two columns are presented showing the various factors influencing the shadow economy with and without the independent variable, 'tax morale'. This table clearly shows how an increase in tax and social security contribution burdens is by far the most important single determinant of the size of the shadow economy. This factor explains 35–38 per cent or 45–52 per cent of the variance of the shadow economy (depending on whether tax morale is included as an independent variable). Tax morale accounts for 22–25 per cent of the variance of the shadow economy.[8] Quality of state institutions accounts for 10–12 per cent and state regulation (mostly of the labour market) accounts for 7–9 per cent.

Tax and social security contributions followed by tax morale and the intensity of state regulations are the major driving forces of the shadow economy. It is worth noting again that these different causes can interact with and reinforce each other. A higher shadow economy can reduce tax revenues and the quality of public services and state institutions; this can raise tax rates and also lower tax morale.

Table 3 **Main causes of the increase of the shadow economy**

Variable	Influence on the shadow economy (in %)*	
	(a)	(b)
Tax and social security contribution burdens	35–38	45–52
Quality of state institutions	10–12	12–17
Labour market regulation	7–9	7–9
Transfer payments	5–7	7–9
Public sector services	5–7	7–9
Tax morale	22–25	–
Influence of all factors	84–98	78–96

(a) Average values of 12 studies
(b) Average values of empirical results of 22 studies
*This is the normalised or standardised influence of the variable average over 12 studies (column a) and 22 studies (column b)
Source: Schneider (2009)

8   The importance of this variable with respect to theory and empirical relevance is also shown in Frey (1997a, 1997b), Feld and Frey (2002a, 2002b, 2007) and Torgler and Schneider (2009).

4 THE SIZE OF THE SHADOW ECONOMY

Statistical estimation of the determinants of the shadow economy

Following the discussion above, we can develop five hypotheses below which will be empirically tested subsequently using the MIMIC approach. The hypotheses are that, all other things being equal:

- An increase in direct and indirect taxation increases the shadow economy.
- An increase in social security contributions increases the shadow economy.
- The higher the level of regulation, the greater the incentives are to work in the shadow economy.
- The lower the quality of state institutions, the greater the incentives are to work in the shadow economy.
- The lower tax morale, the greater the incentives are to work in the shadow economy.

In addition to these hypotheses, it is also reasonable to assume that:

- The higher is unemployment, the more people engage in shadow economy activities.

• The lower GDP per capita is in a country, the higher is the incentive to work in the shadow economy.

These additional variables have been added to the statistical analysis.

In the analysis, we examined a sample of 21 highly developed OECD countries between 1990 and 2007 (with pooled cross-section and time series data). Because the effect of deterrence cannot be empirically tested it is not considered here. The following results correspond to the factors reported in Table 3, which were obtained from an overview of existing studies.

The results in Table 4 use the MIMIC approach to examine the relationship between the shadow economy and various economic variables. Besides the usual cause variables identified in Chapter 3, other variables were added, namely the employment rate, the annual growth rate of GDP and the change of currency per capita. The average working time per week is used as an additional indicator variable.[1] The estimated coefficients of all eight causal variables are statistically significant and have the theoretically expected signs. The tax and social security burden variables are quantitatively the most important ones, followed by the tax morale variable, which has the single biggest influence. Also, quality of state institutions is statistically significant. The development of the official economy measured by unemployment and GDP per capita also has a quantitatively important influence on the shadow economy. Turning to the indicator variables, they all have a statistically significant influence and the estimated coefficients have the expected signs. The quantitatively most important

---

1   This indicator variable might be influenced by state regulation and hence not be truly exogenous.

Table 4 **MIMIC estimation of the shadow economy of 21 highly developed OECD countries, 1990/91, 1994/95, 1997/98, 1999/2000, 2001/02, 2002/03, 2003/04, 2004/05 and 2006/07**

Cause variables	Estimated coefficients
Share of direct taxation	0.392**
(in % of GDP)	(3.34)
Share of indirect taxation	0.184(*)
(in % of GDP)	(1.74)
Share of social security contribution	0.523**
(in % of GDP)	(3.90)
Burden of state regulation (index of labour market regulation, Heritage Foundation, score 1 least regular, score 5 most regular)	0.226(*) (2.03)
Quality of state institutions (rule of law, World Bank, score –3 worst and +3 best case)	–0.314* (–2.70)
Tax morale (WVS and EVS, Index, Scale tax cheating always justified = 1, never justified = 10)	–0.593** (–3.76)
Unemployment rate (%)	0.316**
	(2.40)
GDP per capita (in US$)	–0.106**
	(–3.04)
Indicator variables	**Estimated coefficients**
Employment rate	–0.613**
(in % of population 18–64)	(–2.52)
Average working time (per week)	–1.00 (residual)
Annual growth rate of GDP (adjusted for the mean of all 22 OECD countries)	–0.281**
	(–3.16)
Change in circulation of local currency per capita	0.320**
	(3.80)

Notes: Further details and test statistics are available from the author. t-statistics are in parentheses; (*), *, ** indicate significance at the 90%, 95% and 99% confidence levels respectively.

independent variables are the employment rate and the change in the use of currency per capita.[2]

Summarising, these econometric results suggest that in the OECD countries examined, the social security contributions and the share of direct taxation have the biggest influence on the size of the shadow economy, followed by tax morale and the quality of state institutions.[3] This new examination of the statistical evidence accords strongly with the evidence from previous studies.

The development and size of the shadow economy in Germany

A significant amount of work has been done on the shadow economy in Germany, and this makes an interesting case study before we look at other countries. Various estimates of the German shadow economy (measured as a percentage of official GDP) are shown in Table 5 (see also Feld et al., 2007). The oldest estimate uses the survey method of the Institute for Demoscopy (IfD) in Allensbach, Germany, and shows that the shadow economy was 3.6 per cent of official GDP in 1974. In a much later study, Feld and Larsen (2005, 2008) undertook an extensive research project using the survey method to estimate shadow economic activities in the years 2001 to 2006.[4] Using the officially

2 The variable currency per capita or annual change of currency per capita is heavily influenced by banking innovations or payment; hence this variable can be pretty unstable. Similar problems have already been mentioned by Giles (1999a) and Giles and Tedds (2002).

3 Compare also Schneider et al. (2010) and Feld and Schneider (2010).

4 For a more extensive discussion about the methods used and strengths and weaknesses of the various methods, see Schneider and Enste (2000a), Schneider (2005, 2011), Feld and Larsen (2005, 2008, 2009), Pedersen (2003) and Giles (1999a, 1999b, 1999c).

paid wage rate, they concluded that shadow economic activities reached 4.1 per cent in 2001, 3.1 per cent in 2004, 3.6 per cent in 2005 and 2.5 per cent in 2006.[5] Using the (much lower) shadow economy wage rate these estimates shrink, however, to 1.3 per cent in 2001 and 1.0 per cent in 2004, respectively.

We know, however, that the survey method considerably underestimates the size of the shadow economy. Another approach to estimating the size of the shadow economy in the 1970s and 1980s is the 'discrepancy' approach. This relies on the fact that there are different ways of calculating national income and other aggregate variables (in the case of national income there are the income and expenditure approaches, for example) and that discrepancies between them will, to some extent, reflect shadow economic activity.

The discrepancy approach using national income estimates, and using the discrepancy between official and actual employment estimates of roughly 30 per cent, leads to estimates of the shadow economy of 11 per cent for the 1970s. The physical input methods from which estimates for the 1980s are available suggest values of around 15 per cent for the second half of that decade.

Other methods of estimating the shadow economy also produce much bigger numbers than the survey method. The monetary transaction approach developed by Feige (1989) calculates the shadow economy to have been 30 per cent between 1980 and 1985. The currency demand approach – first used by Kirchgässner (1983, 1984) – provides values of 3.1 per cent in 1970 and

---

5   Feld and Larsen (2008) argue that, owing to the extraordinarily low rate of participation based on a relatively small sample, the results for 2006 must be interpreted with extra care. Additionally it should be noted that these results measure shadow economic activities only in households and not in firms.

Table 5 **The size of the shadow economy in Germany (% of official GDP)**

Method	Shadow economy in Germany ...		
	1970	1975	1980
Survey	–	3.6*	–
	–	–	–
Discrepancy between expenditure and income	11.0	10.2	13.4
Discrepancy between official and actual employment	23.0	38.5	34.0
Physical input method	–	–	–
Transactions approach	17.2	22.3	29.3
Currency demand approach	3.1	6.0	10.3
	12.1	11.8	12.6
	4.5	7.8	9.2
Latent (MIMIC) approach	5.8	6.1	8.2
	–	–	9.4
	4.2	5.8	10.8
Soft modelling	–	8.3*	–

*1974
†2001 and 2005; calculated using wages in the official economy

10.1 per cent for 1980. Kirchgässner's values are quite similar to the ones obtained by Schneider and Enste (2000a, 2002), who also used a currency demand approach to estimate the size of the shadow economy at 4.5 per cent in 1970 and 14.7 per cent in 2000. Estimates using the MIMIC procedures – applied by Frey and Weck-Hannemann (1984) – are quite similar to those from the current demand approach, as are Schneider's estimates also using a MIMIC approach (Schneider 2005, 2009). As noted, the MIMIC estimates have an error margin of +/–15.0 per cent of their estimated value.

| ... (in percentage of official GDP) in: | | | | | Source |
1985	1990	1995	2000	2005	
–	–	–	–	–	IfD Allensbach (1975)
–	–	–	4.1[†]	3.6[†]	Feld and Larsen (2005, 2008)
–	–	–	–	–	Lippert and Walker (1997)
–	–	–	–	–	Langfeldt (1984a, 1984b)
14.5	14.6	–	–	–	Feld and Larsen (2005)
31.4	–	–	–	–	Langfeldt (1984a, 1984b)
–	–	–	–	–	Kirchgässner (1983)
–	–	–	–	–	Langfeldt (1984a, 1984b)
11.3	11.8	12.5	14.7	–	Schneider and Enste (2000a)
–	–	–	–	–	Frey and Weck-Hannemann (1984)
10.1	11.4	15.1	16.3	–	Pickhardt and Sardà Pons (2006)
11.2	12.2	13.9	16.0	15.4	Schneider (2005, 2007)
–	–	–	–	–	Weck-Hannemann (1983)

Thus, one can see that different estimation procedures produce different results. It is safe to say that the figures produced by the transaction and the discrepancy approaches are unrealistically large: the size of the shadow economy at almost one third of official GDP in the mid-1980s is most likely to be an overestimate. The figures obtained using the currency demand and hidden (latent) variable approaches, on the other hand, are relatively close together and much lower than those produced by the discrepancy or transaction approaches. The estimates from the MIMIC approach can be regarded as the most reasonable estimate of the size of the shadow economy, and the survey method is likely to be unrealistically low for the reasons already discussed.

These interpretations can be difficult for economists who are used to trying to measure variables exactly, rather as happens in the physical sciences. The point is that both the survey method and the MIMIC method can help us understand the size and determinants of and the trends in the shadow economy better. Looking at Table 5, it makes sense to make statements such as 'the shadow economy is probably around 10–15 per cent and was growing until 2000' rather than 'the shadow economy was exactly 15.1 per cent in 1995'.

Size and development of the shadow economy in 21 OECD countries

The detailed work on a smaller number of individual countries is important for the estimation of the shadow economy across a broader range of countries. As discussed in Chapter 2, the MIMIC approach can only be used to estimate the relative size of shadow economies. The MIMIC estimation results for the relative sizes of the shadow economy in a broad range of OECD countries, however, can be combined with estimates of the absolute size of the shadow economy using the currency demand approach for Austria, Germany, Italy and the USA (from the studies by Dell'Anno and Schneider, 2003; Bajada and Schneider, 2005; and Schneider and Enste, 2002). Using econometric techniques, it is then possible to estimate the size of the shadow economies in 21 OECD countries as a percentage of national income.[6] Effectively,

---

6   Of course, it is a moot point whether the shadow economy should be measured as a proportion of official national income or as a proportion of official national

the absolute values are used as a form of benchmark procedure to transform the index of the shadow economy from MIMIC estimations into cardinal values.[7]

Table 6 presents these findings for 21 OECD countries until 2007. They clearly reveal that, since the end of 1990s, the size of the shadow economy in most OECD countries has decreased – possibly because there has been some reduction in tax and regulatory burdens in some countries up until 2007. Nevertheless, the estimates are still alarmingly high and the shadow economy grew throughout the 1990s.

The unweighted average for all countries in 1999/2000 was 17 per cent; this dropped to 14 per cent in 2007. This means that since 1997/98 – the year in which the shadow economy was the highest on average in OECD countries – it continually shrank. Only in Germany, Austria and Switzerland did it continue to grow. The reduction of the share of the shadow economy in national income between 1997/98 and 2007 is most pronounced in Italy (a fall of 5 per cent) and in Sweden (a fall of 4 per cent). The fall in government spending and a number of tax rates in recent years in Sweden are particularly notable, so the fall in the size of the shadow economy is not a surprise.

It seems, however, that this fall in the size of the shadow economy stalled or even reversed after 2007. Figures are available only up to 2011 for the European OECD countries. While in some of these European countries (such as France) there was a further modest fall, in others (such as the UK) there has been an

---

income plus the shadow economy (which should give total economic activity). The two different approaches would not change the ordering or the trends in the values and the former approach is used here.

7   This procedure is described in great detail in Dell'Anno and Schneider (2003, 2009).

Table 6 of the shadow economy (% of official GDP) in
         OECD countries

OECD countries	Shadow economy (in % of official GDP)				
	Average 1989/90	Average 1994/95	Average 1997/98	Average 1999	Average 2001
1. Australia	10.1	13.5	14.0	14.4	14.3
2. Austria	6.9	8.6	9.0	10.0	9.7
3. Belgium	19.3	21.5	22.5	22.7	22.1
4. Canada	12.8	14.8	16.2	16.3	15.9
5. Denmark	10.8	17.8	18.3	18.4	18.0
6. Finland	13.4	18.2	18.9	18.4	17.9
7. France	9.0	14.5	14.9	15.7	15.0
8. Germany	11.8	13.5	14.9	16.4	15.9
9. Greece	22.6	28.6	29.0	28.5	28.2
10. Ireland	11.0	15.4	16.2	16.1	15.9
11. Italy	22.8	26.0	27.1	27.8	26.7
12. Japan	8.8	10.6	11.1	11.4	11.2
13. Netherlands	11.9	13.7	13.5	13.3	13.1
14. New Zealand	9.2	11.3	11.9	13.0	12.6
15. Norway	14.8	18.2	19.6	19.2	19.0
16. Portugal	15.9	22.1	23.1	23.0	22.6
17. Spain	16.1	22.4	23.1	23.0	22.4
18. Sweden	15.8	19.5	19.9	19.6	19.1
19. Switzerland	6.7	7.8	8.1	8.8	8.6
20. UK	9.6	12.5	13.0	12.8	12.6
21. USA	6.7	8.8	8.9	8.8	8.8
Unweighted average for 21 OECD countries	12.67	16.16	16.82	17.03	16.65

2003	2005	2007	2009	2011	2012
13.9	13.7	13.5	n/a	n/a	n/a
9.8	9.8	9.5	8.5	8.0	7.6
22.0	21.8	21.3	17.8	17.1	16.8
15.7	15.5	15.3	n/a	n/a	n/a
18.0	17.6	16.9	14.3	13.8	13.4
17.7	17.4	17.0	14.2	13.7	13.3
15.0	14.8	14.7	11.6	11.0	10.8
16.3	16.0	15.3	14.6	13.7	13.3
27.4	26.9	26.5	25.0	24.3	24.0
16.0	15.6	15.4	13.1	12.8	12.7
27.0	27.1	26.8	22.0	21.2	21.6
11.2	10.7	10.3	n/a	n/a	n/a
13.3	13.2	13.0	10.2	9.8	9.5
12.2	12.1	12.0	n/a	n/a	n/a
19.0	18.5	18.0	n/a	n/a	n/a
23.0	23.3	23.0	19.5	19.4	19.4
22.4	22.4	22.2	19.5	19.2	19.2
18.7	18.6	17.9	15.4	14.7	14.3
8.8	8.5	8.1	n/a	n/a	n/a
12.5	12.4	12.2	10.9	11.0	10.3
8.7	8.5	8.4	n/a	n/a	n/a
16.6	16.4	16.06	n/a	n/a	n/a

increase since 2007. The financial crash and subsequent recession are possible explanations for this. Unemployment has risen and jobs in the formal economy have been more difficult to obtain. In addition, tax rates have risen as governments have tried to reduce budget deficits.

The German shadow economy is in the middle of the ranking of OECD countries, whereas Austria and Switzerland are at the lower end. Southern European countries have the biggest shadow economies (20–26 per cent of official national income). Indeed, each of Portugal, Spain, Italy and Greece have shadow economic activity equal to between about one fifth and one quarter of the official economy. Scandinavian countries have shadow economies that are above the average for OECD countries. This is interesting because Nordic countries are often characterised as having a high degree of equality which, it is suggested, gives rise to a high level of trust and good social norms. They also have very high tax burdens, however (though often a relatively light regulatory burden).

One of the reasons for the differences in the size of the shadow economy between OECD countries is the level of regulation. For example, there are fewer regulations in the USA compared with Germany, where everything is forbidden that is not explicitly allowed. In Germany, individual freedom is limited in many areas by far-reaching state intervention. Indeed, even in the USA it is worth noting that one large area of shadow economic activity (not examined separately in this study) is in relation to the work of illegal immigrants – immigration is one policy area that is heavily regulated in the USA and the consequences are clear. Another reason for the differences between the sizes of the shadow economy in the USA and Switzerland and other OECD countries is the level of taxation. The direct and indirect tax burden was the lowest in the USA and Switzerland among OECD countries for most of this period. The size of the shadow economy in the UK is a little below the OECD average at 10.6 per cent and was just one percentage point higher at the end of the period than at the beginning.

Development and size of the shadow economies throughout the world[8]

Figure 1 shows, in summary form, the average size of the shadow economy of 162 countries over the period 1999–2007.[9] Table 7 shows the average size of the shadow economy in different regions, as defined by the World Bank. The World Bank distinguishes eight world regions, which are: East Asia and Pacific; Europe (non-OECD) and Central Asia; Latin America and the Caribbean; Middle East and North Africa; high-income OECD;[10] other high-income countries; South Asia; and sub-Saharan Africa.

If we consider the average size of the shadow economies of these regions weighted by total GDP in 2005, sub-Saharan Africa has the highest with 37.6 per cent, followed by Europe (non-OECD) and Central Asia with 36.4 per cent and Latin America and the Caribbean with 34.7 per cent. The lowest level of shadow economic activity is in high-income OECD countries with 13.4 per cent. The average size of the shadow economy throughout the world, weighted by national income, is 17.1 per cent. The unweighted average is 33 per cent over the period 1999–2007.

8   This part and the figures are taken from Schneider et al. (2010).
9   In Appendix 2 a list of these 162 countries is shown in alphabetical order.
10   The numbers for OECD countries are slightly different from the analysis above, which contained only a subset of OECD countries.

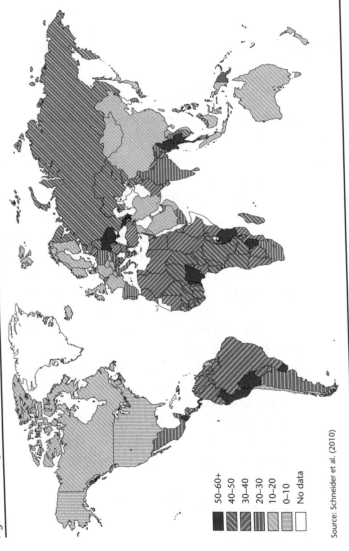

Figure 1　Average size of the shadow economy of 162 countries, 1999–2007

50–60+
40–50
30–40
20–30
10–20
0–10
No data

Source: Schneider et al. (2010)

Table 7 **Average size of informal/shadow economy weighted by total GDP of 2005**

	Region	Mean	Median	Min	Max	Standard deviation
EAP	East Asia and Pacific	17.5	12.7	12.7	50.6	10.6
ECA	Europe and Central Asia	36.4	32.6	18.1	65.8	8.4
LAC	Latin America and the Caribbean	34.7	33.8	19.3	66.1	7.9
MENA	Middle East and North Africa	27.3	32.5	18.3	37.2	7.7
OECD	High-Income OECD	13.4	11.0	8.5	28.0	5.7
OHIE	Other High-Income	20.8	19.4	12.4	33.4	4.9
SAS	South Asia	25.1	22.2	22.2	43.9	5.9
SSA	Sub-Saharan Africa	37.6	33.2	18.4	61.8	11.7
World		17.1	13.2	8.5	66.1	9.9

Source: Schneider et al. (2010)

It is worth noting that, in many parts of the world, the shadow economy is more or less endemic and is often described simply as 'informal' rather than 'shadow'. Such informal activity does not take place because individuals are deliberately avoiding paying taxes and avoiding abiding by regulation but because the infrastructure does not exist for the effective and efficient registration of businesses and to ensure the efficient collection of taxes. In many poorer countries, the shadow economy is not so much a problem of evasion by citizens but of an inability of people to pay taxes and register their activity even if they would wish to do so.[11]

---

11   The work of Hernando de Soto on this topic is particularly telling.

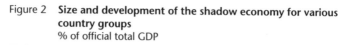

Figure 2 **Size and development of the shadow economy for various country groups**
% of official total GDP

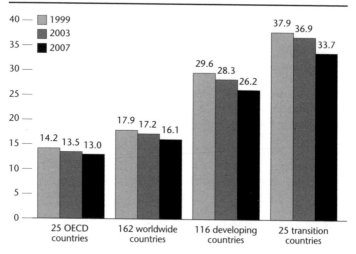

Source: Schneider et al. (2010)

Informal economic activity may also be tolerated to a high degree and in some sectors, such as agriculture, not even be regarded as a policy issue. It follows from this that the policies that one might adopt to tackle the informal economy might be very different in countries where legal infrastructure is lacking compared with where the infrastructure exists but is deliberately – and illegally – ignored by those working in the shadow economy.

There has been a general reduction in the size of the shadow economy over time. In Figure 2, the size and development of the shadow economy of various country groups through the years 1999, 2003 and 2007 are shown. These figures are averages weighted by the level of official GDP in 2005. It is clear that, for all the country groups (25 OECD countries, 116 developing countries, 25 transition countries), there is a decrease in the size of the shadow economy. The average size of the shadow economies of the 162 countries was 34 per cent of official GDP[12] in 1999, and this decreased to a little over 31 per cent of official GDP in 2007 (see also Table 27 in Appendix 2). This is a decrease of almost three percentage points over nine years. The growth of the official economy with reduced unemployment and increased formal employment seems to be the most efficient means to reduce the shadow economy in many parts of the world.

---

12   This is unweighted.

5 THE SHADOW ECONOMY LABOUR MARKET

Introduction

Having examined the size, rise and fall of the shadow economy in terms of value added over time, in this chapter we now specifically look in more detail at the shadow labour market.

Illicit work can take many forms. The underground use of labour may consist of a second job after (or even during) regular working hours. A second form is shadow economy work by individuals who do not participate in the official labour market. A third component is the employment of people such as illegal immigrants who are not allowed to work in the official economy. Empirical research on the shadow economy labour market is even more difficult than research on the value added in the whole shadow economy because it is difficult to determine how many hours an average shadow economy worker is actually working. Shadow economy work can involve anything from a full-time shadow economy job or self-employment without payment of taxes to a few hours of child-minding or bar work every two or three weeks.[1]

To understand the shadow labour market, it is worth asking

---

[1]   For developing countries some literature about the shadow labour market exists: Dallago (1990), Pozo (1996), Loayza (1996), Chickering and Salahdine (1991) and OECD (2009a).

why people work in the shadow economy. In the official labour market, the costs that firms and individuals have to incur when hiring somebody are increased by the burden of tax and social insurance payments, as well as by regulation. In some OECD countries, these costs are greater than the wage effectively earned by the worker – providing a strong incentive to work in the shadow economy.

Reliable and consistent information on total non-wage costs is difficult to obtain and non-wage costs can vary depending on the level of pay, benefits being received and other factors. As such, averages do not necessarily indicate the incentives that are faced by specific groups when deciding to work in the shadow economy. Nevertheless, Table 8 shows non-wage costs for a selection of OECD countries for people in the bottom half of the earnings spectrum.

Table 8 **Non-wage costs, selected OECD countries, for individuals in the bottom half of the earnings spectrum**

Country	Non-wage costs, 2010	Low-wage trap for one-earner couple with two children, 2010
Germany	45%	80%
Sweden	41%	77%
United Kingdom	30%	79%
EU average	39%	58%
USA	28%	68%
Switzerland	18%	n/a

Source: http://epp.eurostat.ec.europa.eu/statistics_explained/index.
php?title=File:Tax_rate_indicators_on_low_wage_earners,_2005_and_2010_(%25).
png

Non-wage costs in this case are defined as income tax on gross wage earnings plus employee and employer social security contributions, expressed as a percentage of total labour costs. The measure therefore ignores costs of regulation and also value added tax, which might be relevant for sole traders in particular. The figures in Table 8 relate to low earners (those receiving 67 per cent of average earnings in the business economy). It can be seen that there is a very high level of non-wage costs in many countries – especially in the European Union. This makes shadow economic activity more attractive. The burden of those non-wage costs can, of course, be borne by either the employer or the employee, depending on the dynamics of the labour market. The size of these non-wage costs, however, will clearly provide incentives for the employee or the employer – or both – to agree to informal work.

The low wage trap measures the percentage of gross earnings which is 'taxed away' through the combined effects of income taxes, social security contributions, and any withdrawal of benefits when gross earnings increase from 33 per cent to 67 per cent of the average earnings of a worker in the business economy. The figures relate specifically to single-earner couples with two children between six and eleven years old. This figure – which in many EU countries is around 80 per cent – is also highly relevant. If individuals in such families earn a low wage in the formal economy, they will have a much stronger incentive to increase their take-home pay by working in the shadow economy than by working in the formal economy. This helps to explain why so many people work in the shadow economy in addition to having low-paid work in the formal economy.

It is clear that there are very strong monetary incentives to work in the shadow economy. The detailed work on the labour supply decision suggests that this is important in explaining behaviour. Lemieux et al. (1994) use micro-data from a survey conducted in Quebec City in Canada. Their study provides economic insights regarding the size of the distortion caused by income tax and the welfare system. The results of this study suggest that hours worked in the shadow economy are responsive to changes in the net wage in the official sector. Indeed, the substitution between labour market activities in the formal and shadow sectors is high. These empirical findings indicate: 'participation rates and hours worked in the underground sector also tend to be inversely related to the number of hours worked in the regular sector' (ibid.: 235). These findings demonstrate a large negative elasticity of hours worked in the shadow economy with respect to the wage rate in the formal sector and also demonstrate high mobility between the sectors.

Kucera and Roncolato (2008: 321) also deal with informal employment. They address intensive labour market regulations as a major cause of informal employment and so-called 'voluntary' informal employment. The authors give a theoretical overview of both issues and also a survey of a number of empirical studies in which the effect of official labour market regulations on informal employment is analysed. They find a significant and quantitatively important influence. These issues will be discussed further below.

The remainder of this chapter looks at the shadow labour force in Denmark and Germany (two case studies on which extensive work has been published) and then widens the discussion to include other OECD countries. The problem is then examined from the point of view of developing and transition countries before data is disaggregated for further analysis. As will be discussed, the nature of the 'shadow' economy is different in developed from developing countries. Often, in developing countries, informal employment without proper recognised contracts of employment and without payment of taxes is the norm – especially in rural areas. Informal employment may be taken not to avoid taxes but because the legal systems are such that formal employment is extremely difficult to arrange. As such, the term 'shadow employment' – which is perhaps inappropriate to describe such situations – will generally be reserved for developed countries where tax evasion is often the main aim. The term 'informal' will generally be used below to describe employment without formal contracts, the payment of taxes and so on in developing countries.

Two micro-studies of the shadow economy labour market

In this section we examine case studies about the size and development of shadow economy labour markets in Denmark and in Germany.[2]

Micro-study of Denmark

Hvidtfeldt et al. (2011) investigated the size and development of undeclared work in Denmark over the years 2008–10. They claim that more than half of all Danes purchase undeclared work in the

---

2   The selection of these two studies is based on the fact that they use data from 2010 and both provide important and detailed insights into why people choose to demand and supply shadow work. Compare also Feld and Larsen (2005, 2008, 2009) and Schneider (2011).

course of a year. The authors obtained this finding from an interview survey of 2,200 Danes conducted by the Rockwool Foundation Research Unit in 2010. According to their survey, 52 per cent of those questioned had purchased undeclared work in the previous year and had paid in cash, in kind or through the provision of return services. Their survey also showed that an additional 28 per cent of Danes would be willing to buy undeclared services, even though they had not actually done so within the previous year. In total, 80 per cent of the Danish population are potential customers for undeclared work and only 20 per cent said that they would refuse to pay for work undertaken in the shadow economy.

Table 9 shows the proportions of Danish men carrying out undeclared work in 2010 in different sectors. It can be seen that shadow economy work is particularly prevalent in certain sectors. Nearly 50 per cent have carried out undeclared work in the construction sector and a similar figure in agriculture and motor vehicle sales and repairs. On average nearly one third of Danish men carried out shadow economy work.

In this study, the authors also examine undeclared work over a fifteen-year period since 1994. They come to the conclusion that Danes now do approximately as much undeclared work today as they did fifteen years ago. The latest figures from 2008–10 show that every fourth adult Dane carried out some kind of undeclared work in the course of a year, with men and younger people being more inclined to shadow economic activity than women and older people. Those involved in shadow economic activity spent around three hours per week working in the shadow sector, a figure which has also remained unchanged since 1994. The proportion of undeclared work in relation to national income has remained

Table 9 **Proportions of men who had carried out undeclared work in the previous twelve months**

Sector	Percentage carrying out undeclared work
Building and construction	48
Agriculture (incl. gardening), fishing and mineral extraction	47
Motor vehicle sales and repairs	43
Energy and water supply	(38)
Manufacturing	36
Transport and telecommunications	31
Hotel and restaurant	(30)
Financial and business services	28
Public and personal services	26
Retail, wholesale and repair (excluding motor vehicles)	26
OVERALL	32

Note: Figures in parentheses are based on fewer than 50 observations.
Source: Hvidtfeldt et al. (2011: 5)

a little below 3 per cent throughout the period. This, of course, is a measure of shadow economic activity which excludes much of the activity discussed in earlier chapters and which relies on surveys that tend to understate the amount of shadow work. The interesting aspect of these findings, however, is not so much the level of the shadow economy in terms of the value of goods and services produced but how widespread shadow economic activity is among those working and purchasing goods and services.

The Danish survey also found wide acceptance of the shadow economy, especially for those earning relatively small amounts of money. As Tables 10 and 11 show, over 80 per cent of the population would find it acceptable for somebody to have undeclared income if they were doing undeclared work worth only £20 a week but only 27 per cent would find it acceptable if a skilled tradesman earned £5,000 a year from undeclared work.

Table 10 **Proportion of the Danish population who find it acceptable that a schoolgirl should earn undeclared income for babysitting, 2007/08**

If she earns DKK200 per week	84%
If she earns DKK300 per week	70%

Note: The sterling:krone exchange rate was approximately 1:10.
Source: Hvidtfeldt et al. (2011: 14)

Table 11 **Proportion of the Danish population who find it acceptable that a skilled tradesman should earn undeclared income, 2007/08**

If he earns DKK10,000 per year	47%
If he earns DKK50,000 per year	27%

Note: The sterling:krone exchange rate was approximately 1:10.
Source: Hvidtfeldt et al. (2011: 14)

It is interesting that Danes tolerate shadow economy earnings from those earning a small amount from the shadow economy to a significantly greater degree than they tolerate those earning much greater amounts. The level of toleration is generally high, however, something that is not surprising given the proportion of Danes who admit to purchasing shadow economic services.

Micro-study of Germany

The shadow labour market in Germany has been investigated by Haigner et al. (2011). They use data from a representative survey of 2,104 German residents conducted in May 2010. The usual caveats about survey data of the shadow economy apply. In order to encourage more honest answers, however, the interviewees were read the following text (translated from German):

> The next set of questions deals with what is called shadow work. We survey these questions on behalf of a group of independent scientists, who will process the results within a study. By black work they mean the following: somebody who works for somebody and agrees not to pay taxes for the payment. In this case, both partners are better off because no value added tax, income tax or social security contributions are paid. Such procedures are frequently occurring, for example, in cleaning, gardening, baby-sitting, waiting at table, writing or programming. Also, work which is not taxed is prevalent in construction, renovation, car repair and taking care of elderly people.

Moreover, if interviewers recognised that the interviewees hesitated to answer the questions on shadow labour supply and demand, they would again explain that the interview was confidential and that answers were confidential, anonymous and only for scientific use. The question on shadow labour supply was (translated from German): 'Have you, during the last year, worked for somebody in the way described above (black work)?' Questions were also asked of those potentially using workers from the shadow economy. The question on shadow labour demand was (again translated from German): 'Have you, during the last year, demanded black work?' Moreover, the researchers asked shadow labour suppliers the reasons for working in the shadow economy; the time when they undertook such work (working time, weekends, vacations, and so on); the sector in which they worked; the number of hours they worked per month; and the estimated hourly wage they received.

In order to understand the general attitudes towards shadow labour supply and demand, survey respondents were asked to declare their views in accordance with a set of thirteen statements on the topic. The results were interesting. There was considerable awareness of the fact that shadow labour reduces the tax revenues of the state. People also claimed, however, that high tax rates made working in the shadow economy more attractive. Interestingly, many people suggested that they liked shadow labour because it was more rapidly available and more flexible than official labour, which was widely perceived to be subject to strict regulations. Moreover, people in general did not agree with the statement that shadow labour suppliers should be reported to the police, nor would many people have reported them to the police themselves. This shows that shadow labour in Germany is perceived as a rather trivial offence. The strongest positive answers were to the proposition that labour faces regulations that are too strict and that shadow labour was cheaper than formal labour.

Out of 2,104 respondents, 285 (14 per cent) declared that they were supplying shadow labour during the year before the survey. Among men, the fraction of shadow labour suppliers was significantly higher (19 per cent) than among women (9 per cent). Moreover, the authors found above-average proportions supplying shadow labour among the unemployed (30 per cent) and among people out of the labour force 'owing to other reasons' (24 per cent). Among pensioners (5 per cent) and homemakers (10 per cent) the proportion is below average, while it is close to average among students (14 per cent), apprentices (12 per cent),

Figure 3   **Percentage of shadow labour engaged in different sectors**

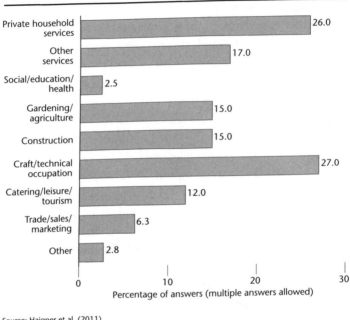

Source: Haigner et al. (2011)

self-employed persons (15 per cent) and dependent employees (16 per cent). Among persons who have not completed compulsory education and those who have completed an apprenticeship, shadow labour suppliers are over-represented (24 per cent and 20 per cent respectively), while they are under-represented among persons with a university degree (7 per cent).

Figure 3 shows the sectors in which shadow work is taking place. Not surprisingly, crafts and technical occupations and private household services have the highest relative importance. More than a quarter of shadow labour is engaged in these areas.

Figure 4   **Reasons for supplying shadow labour**

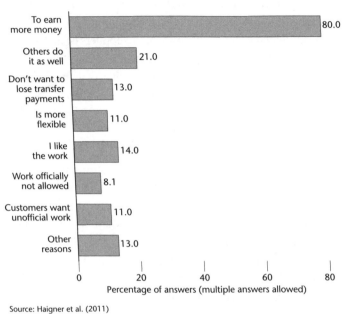

Percentage of answers (multiple answers allowed)

Source: Haigner et al. (2011)

The proportions in Figure 3 do not add up to 100 per cent since multiple answers were allowed.

The authors also asked those survey respondents who engaged in shadow labour supply their reasons for doing so. The results are reported in Figure 4. Four out of five supply shadow labour in order to earn more money – though this does not really address the question of why such people work in the shadow rather than the formal sector. About one in eight shadow labour suppliers do so because they do not want to lose transfer payments. In the German social system, pensions, as well as unemployment benefit and social assistance payments, are cut when people earn more and implicit marginal tax and benefit withdrawal rates can be more than 100 per cent in the official labour market.

More than one in five shadow labour suppliers claim that their motive is that others do it as well. This result is in line with the finding above that German residents perceive, in general, shadow labour supply and demand to be a rather trivial offence.

The shadow labour force in OECD countries

Table 12 shows estimates for the shadow economy labour force in a number of OECD countries (Austria, Denmark, France, Germany, Italy, Spain and Sweden). There are no reliable estimates beyond the end of the 1990s except where specific country studies have been undertaken (see above), and in some cases ranges have been suggested given the uncertainties involved in estimation. The shadow labour force is high relative to the formal labour force and has also generally increased. For example, in Denmark the shadow economy labour force grew from 8.3 per cent in 1980 to 15.4 per cent in 1997/98. In Germany, there was also a considerable rise, from 8–12 per cent in 1974 to 19–22 per cent in 1997/98. Estimates of the shadow labour force in Italy vary from 30 to 48 per cent for 1997/98. Spain and Sweden also have very high values. In the EU as a whole about thirty million people were engaged in shadow economy activities in 1997/98 and in all European OECD countries it is estimated that 48 million people work illicitly.[3]

---

3   Note that the EU was much smaller in 1997/98.

Table 12 **Estimates of the size of the shadow economy labour force in selected OECD countries, 1974–98**

Country	Year	Shadow economy labour force in 1,000s*	Shadow economy participants, % of official labour force[†]	Sources
Austria	1990/91	300–380	9.6	Schneider (1998a,
	1997/98	500–750	16.0	1998b) and
				own calculations
Denmark	1980	250	8.3	Mogensen et al.
	1986	390	13.0	(1995)
	1991	410	14.3	and own calculations
	1994	420	15.4	
France	1975–82	800–1,500	3.0–6.0	De Grazia (1983)
	1997/98	1,400–3,200	6.0–12.0	and
				own calculations
Germany	1974–82	3,000–4,000	8.0–12.0	De Grazia (1983),
	1997/98	7,000–9,000	19.0–23.0	Schneider (1998a,
				1998b) and own
				calculations
Italy	1979	4,000–7,000	20.0–35.0	Gaetani-d'Aragona
	1997/98	6,600–11,400	30.0–48.0	(1979) and
				own calculations
Spain	1979/80	1,250–3,500	9.6–26.5	Ruesga (1984) and
	1997/98	1,500–4,200	11.5–32.3	own calculations
Sweden	1978	750	13.0–14.0	De Grazia (1983)
	1997/98	1,150	19.8	and own calculations
European Union	1978	15 million		De Grazia (1983)
	1997/98	30 million		and own calculations
OECD (Europe)	1978	26 million		De Grazia (1983)
	1997/98	48 million[§]		and own calculations

*Estimated full-time jobs equivalent including unregistered workers, illegal immigrants and second jobs.
†Percentage of population aged 20–69, survey method.
§These figures are totals.
Source: OECD, Paris, various years

75

Table 13 **Full-time equivalent shadow economy workers and illegal foreign workers in Germany, Austria and Switzerland, 1995–2009***

Year	Germany		Austria		Switzerland	
	Shadow economy workers ('000)	Illegal foreign workers ('000)	Shadow economy workers ('000)	Illegal foreign workers ('000)	Shadow economy workers ('000)	Illegal foreign workers ('000)
1995	7,320	878	575	75	391	55
1996	7,636	939	617	83	426	61
1997	7,899	987	623	86	456	67
1998	8,240	1,039	634	89	462	69
1999	8,524	1,074	667	93	484	74
2000	8,621	1,103	703	99	517	79
2001	8,909	1,149	734	104	543	84
2002	9,182	1,194	746	109	556	88
2003	9,420	1,225	769	112	565	90
2004	9,023	1,103	789	114	560	89
2005	8,549	1,002	750	104	520	82
2006	8,124	952	716	98	493	78
2007	8,206	961	709	97	490	77
2008	8,154	955	679	93	471	74
2009	8,272	968	713	98	484	76

*Numbers calculated using total hours worked and then transformed into full-time equivalent jobs. Most people who work in the shadow economy are part-time shadow economy workers. Illegal foreign workers are approximated from the number of detected illegal foreign workers.
Source: Own calculations, 2010

These figures demonstrate that the shadow economy labour market is large and this may provide an explanation of why one can observe such high and persistent unemployment in the EU – there may be significant shadow labour market activity. It is also notable that the estimates for the proportion of shadow economy workers (as a proportion of the full-time workforce) are not very different from the estimates of shadow economy output (as a proportion of total output). Though the methods of measurement are different and different measurement errors might be involved in both sets of calculations, this indicates that productivity in the shadow economy is roughly as high as in the official economy. More generally, these results demonstrate that the shadow economy labour force has reached a remarkable size in highly developed European OECD countries.

In Table 13, data are shown for later years for three countries and also to illustrate the specific problem of illegal migration. Data are very scarce in this field for other countries. Once again, the data are for full-time equivalent workers, though the vast majority of shadow economy workers work part time. In Germany, the number of full-time equivalent shadow economy workers was about seven million in 1995, and this had increased to 8.2 million in 2009. There were around one million illegal foreign-born full-time equivalent workers throughout this period. For all three countries, illegal foreign-born workers were only a relatively small proportion of the shadow economy labour force.

The relationship between self-employment and the shadow economy is also a potentially important area for policy. In some countries, such as the UK, self-employment exists as a separate formal tax status and has some tax advantages. These tax advantages arise partly because social security contributions (which are reduced for the self-employed) are not closely related to benefits that people obtain from the system. This situation, together with the costs and regulations imposed on small businesses employing people, can lead to high levels of self-employment but where the work undertaken is all within the formal economy.

At the same time, self-employment can give rise to easier opportunities for shadow employment. Thus, for example, a self-employed tradesman can relatively easily not declare certain income for certain jobs where cash payments are made. There certainly seems to be a relationship between the proportion of self-employed as a proportion of total employment and the size of the shadow economy. From EU OECD countries, Greece (48 per cent), Poland (26 per cent) and Italy (25 per cent) all have especially high levels of self-employment and large shadow economies. As will be discussed in later chapters, this makes it especially important that there are minimal regulatory barriers to small businesses registering formally and to businesses taking on employees.

The informal labour force in developing and transition economies

As has been noted, the size and nature of the informal economy vary widely internationally. Perhaps more importantly, however, the underlying motivation for informal work also varies widely.

Estimates of the informal economy labour force worldwide are based on the OECD and World Bank database of informal employment in major cities and in rural areas, as well as on other sources (see footnotes). The values are calculated in absolute terms and as a percentage of the official labour force, assuming that the informal economy in rural areas is at least as high as in the cities. This is a conservative assumption, since in reality it is likely to be even larger.[4] Survey techniques and, for some coun-

---

4   The assumption that the shadow economy labour force is at least as high in rural areas as in major cities is a very modest one. That this is so is supported by Lubell

tries, the MIMIC method and the method of the discrepancy between the official and actual labour force are used for estimation. The results are therefore not entirely consistent across very different countries and should be regarded as indications of the size of the informal sector. Data for informal employment are not full-time equivalents but represent the total number involved in informal employment whether full time or part time.

A recent OECD study (OECD, 2009a)[5] concludes that, in many parts of the world, informal employment is the norm, not the exception,. More than half of all jobs in the non-agricultural sectors of developing countries – over 0.9 billion workers – can be considered informal. If agricultural workers in developing countries are included, this leads to an estimate of around two billion people. Most informal workers in the developing world are self-employed and work independently or they own and manage very small enterprises. According to the OECD study (ibid.), informal employment is a result both of people being excluded from official jobs and people voluntarily opting out of formal structures. In many middle-income countries incentives drive individuals and businesses out of the formal sector – formal employment is practically very difficult to find.

Hernando de Soto, for example, has investigated this phenomenon for many middle-income countries. Though the situation in Peru – where the original fieldwork was undertaken – has changed

(1991). Some authors (e.g. Lubell, 1991, Pozo, 1996 and Chickering and Salahdine, 1991) argue that the illicit labour force is nearly twice as high in the countryside as in urban areas. But since no (precise) data exists on this ratio, the assumption of an equal size may be justified arguing that such a calculation provides a lower bound for the size of the shadow economy.

5   The following results and figures are taken from the OECD (2009a) executive summary.

somewhat, the general problem remains the same. De Soto (2000) showed how, on average, 15 per cent of turnover in Peruvian manufacturing businesses was paid out in bribes. This was done because the alternative of registering the business legally was so expensive. For a business to become legal and register its property in Lima it took over three hundred working days at a cost of 32 times the monthly minimum wage. The 2010 World Bank *Doing Business* report points out that African countries have an average rank of 139 in the world for ease of doing business compared with the average rank for OECD countries of 30. It is often the obstacles to doing business legally which lead to so much informal economic activity. If businesses cannot register legally, they cannot take on employees with formal contracts and with the appropriate legal arrangements with the tax authorities. This is quite a different problem from that of using the shadow economy to evade taxes.

Compared with just under two billion people who work in the informal sector, only 1.2 billion people have formal contracts of employment and social security protection globally. In some regions, the picture is even more dramatic. Informal economic activity, excluding the agricultural sector, accounts for three-quarters of jobs in sub-Saharan Africa, more than two-thirds in South and South-East Asia, half in Latin America, the Middle East and North Africa, and nearly one quarter in transition countries. As noted, estimates suggest that, if agriculture is included, the size of the informal economy in the above-mentioned regions is even higher (for example, more than 90 per cent in South Asia).

In addition, this OECD study concludes that more than 700 million informal workers have an income of less than $1.25 a day and 1.2 billion earn less than $2 a day. The share of informal employment also tends to increase during economic turmoil. For example, during the Argentinian economic crisis (1999–2002), the country's official economy shrank by almost one fifth while the share of informal employment expanded from 48 to 52 per cent.

Developing countries – early studies[6]

The size of the informal labour force in African countries during the 1990s is shown in Table 14. Gambia had the largest informal economy labour force as a proportion of the official labour force at 80 per cent, followed by Guinea with 79 per cent, Benin with 77 per cent, Rwanda with 75 per cent and the Republic of Congo with 50 per cent.[7] Zimbabwe had the lowest rate of informal work with 34 per cent of the official labour force. For African countries, the figures show considerable variation and should really be seen as preliminary results or indications of the real size of the informal sector. If it is assumed that the informal labour force is as productive as the official economy and contributes per capita a similar added value, the informal economy national income can be calculated, which is also shown in Table 14. On average, the supply of illicit work in these 33 African countries was 54 per cent of the official labour force and 25 per cent of the population.

6 This section is adapted from Schneider and Enste (2002: part 5, pp. 43–51).

7 These high values strongly indicate that a considerable number of these illicit workers also have (at least part-time) jobs in the official economy. Yet the number of these 'double-job-holders' is unknown and may differ from country to country. Given this, the ratio of the shadow economy labour force as a percentage of the official labour force should be interpreted very cautiously, since it is unclear what this ratio actually stands for. Hence interpretation is very difficult. In addition, making comparisons between different countries is very complicated and such comparisons provide only a very crude picture. Arguably, the rate of the shadow economy labour force as a percentage of the population is a somewhat better gauge.

Table 14 **Informal economy labour force in Africa, 1998**

Country	millions	% of official labour force	% of population	Informal national income as % of official national income
Angola	1.90	35.7	16.3	16.2
Benin	2.00	76.9	34.5	34.5
Botswana	0.30	45.0	19.6	19.3
Burkina Faso	3.40	65.0	32.5	31.4
Cameroon	3.50	61.7	25.1	24.5
Chad	1.30	38.0	18.2	n/a
Congo	0.60	50.3	22.1	21.8
Côte d'Ivoire	3.40	60.3	23.9	23.6
Dem. Rep. of Congo	15.70	80.0	33.6	32.0
Ethiopia	15.70	61.0	26.3	25.3
Gabon	0.30	58.0	26.1	n/a
Gambia	0.50	80.0	42.4	41.2
Ghana	6.10	72.3	33.9	33.0
Guinea	2.60	79.0	37.6	36.9
Kenya	6.00	40.8	21.0	21.4
Lesotho	0.31	38.8	15.4	15.4
Liberia	0.40	35.0	13.8	n/a
Madagascar	3.90	57.5	27.6	27.4
Malawi	2.50	51.7	24.3	23.8
Mali	1.80	36.0	17.5	17.3
Mauritania	0.50	41.0	20.3	20.5
Namibia	0.33	47.1	20.4	20.4
Niger	2.30	51.0	23.5	n/a
Nigeria	23.40	48.9	19.8	48.8
Rwanda	3.20	75.0	40.5	38.7
Senegal	2.50	62.4	28.4	27.6
Sierra Leone	1.30	70.0	27.4	25.9
Sudan	4.60	42.6	16.3	16.3
Tanzania	6.80	42.2	21.7	21.7
Togo	0.70	38.9	16.1	16.1
Tunisia	2.00	57.1	21.5	21.5
Uganda	5.80	56.4	28.5	n/a
Zimbabwe	1.80	33.9	15.7	15.7
Average of 33 countries	3.9	54.2	24.6	25.7

Table 15 illustrates the equivalent results for a selection of Asian countries. In China, it was estimated that 160 million people worked in the informal economy – 22 per cent of the official labour force. This figure should be interpreted with care given that the country is communist; it is not surprising, however, that a communist country should have a smaller informal labour force than other developing economies. In India, just over two hundred million people worked illicitly – around 50 per cent of the official labour force. In Indonesia, the third-most populous country in this group, 36.7 million people were engaged in informal economic activities; this corresponds to 37 per cent of the official labour force. In Pakistan, around thirty million people or 60 per cent of the official labour force worked in the informal economy. The high level of informal economic activity in Asia is also confirmed by the OECD (2009a) study. On the whole, the informal economy labour force in these Asian countries made up 47 per cent of the official labour force and 20 per cent of the population.

The size of the informal labour force in a selection of South American states is shown in Table 16 for 1998. In absolute terms, Brazil had the highest informal economy labour force with 37.4 million (49 per cent of the official labour force), followed by Colombia with 9.7 million (54 per cent). Both Ecuador (with 59 per cent) and Peru (55 per cent) had a similar rate of informal working. Chile had the lowest rate, with 40 per cent of the official labour force. Overall, the informal economy labour force in these nine countries was 50 per cent of the size of the official labour force and 20 per cent of the population.

Table 15 **Informal economy labour force in Asia, 1998**

Country	Informal employment (1998)			Informal national income as % of official national income
	millions	As % of labour force	As % of population	
China	162.40	21.9	13.1	13.1
India	217.20	50.4	22.2	22.4
Indonesia	36.70	37.4	18.0	11.3
Mongolia	0.42	44.0	16.2	16.9
Nepal	8.60	78.1	37.6	37.6
Pakistan	29.40	60.0	22.3	n/a
Philippines	9.80	30.6	13.0	13.1
Sri Lanka	2.50	31.3	13.3	n/a
Yemen	3.30	65.0	19.9	22.5
Average of 9 countries	52.3	46.5	19.5	19.5

Source: Own calculations based on World Bank, World Development Indicators, http://www.worldbank.org/html/extdr/regions.htm

Transition countries – early studies

The informal economy in nine transition countries has also been analysed (see Table 17). The highest level of informal activity was in Armenia (76 per cent of the official labour force), followed by Croatia with 70 per cent and Bulgaria with 63 per cent. In aggregate, well over one hundred million people were working in the shadow economy in these countries. Slovenia had the lowest informal labour force with 31 per cent of the official labour force. On average, the shadow economy labour force in these nine transition countries was 49 per cent of the official labour force and 24 per cent of the population. Here the findings should be interpreted with great care, as these transition countries switched

Table 16 **Informal economy labour force in Latin and South America, 1998**

Country	millions	% of labour force	% of population	Informal national income as % of official national income
Bolivia	1.54	51.3	19.5	20.8
Brazil	37.40	49.2	22.5	n/a
Chile	2.40	40.0	16.2	15.7
Colombia	9.70	53.8	23.8	23.8
Ecuador	2.94	58.8	24.1	24.1
El Salvador	1.40	47.3	23.0	23.1
Guatemala	2.01	50.3	18.6	19.6
Paraguay	0.80	41.0	15.4	15.3
Peru	4.91	54.6	19.8	19.8
Average of 9 countries	7.0	49.6	20.3	20.3

Source: Schneider and Enste (2002: ch. 5), based on World Bank, World Development Indicators, http://www.worldbank.org/html/extdr/regions.htm

from a planned economy to a market economy and, owing to this, official statistics are not very accurate and calculation methods are approximate. These results are not a surprise, however. A move from a centrally planned to a freer economy often leads to a situation whereby shadow economic activity is more acceptable and the legal infrastructure for regulation, taxation and so on is often very inadequate in the early stages of transition. Indeed, such shadow economy work should not necessarily be regarded as a bad thing.

Table 17 **Informal economy labour force in a selection of transition countries, 1998**

Country	millions	% of labour force	% of population	Informal national income as % of official national income
Armenia	1.51	75.5	39.7	40.3
Bulgaria	2.52	63.0	30.4	30.7
Croatia	1.40	70.0	31.1	30.6
Georgia	1.10	36.7	20.4	20.1
Kazakhstan	2.80	40.0	17.9	18.9
Kyrgyzstan	0.80	40.0	17.0	17.5
Romania	4.70	42.7	20.9	20.9
Russian Federation	32.9	42.2	22.4	22.4
Slovenia	0.31	31.0	15.5	15.6
Average of all countries (unweighted)		49.0	23.9	24.1

Source: Schneider and Enste (2002: ch. 5), based on World Bank, *World Development Indicators*, http://www.worldbank.org/html/extdr/regions.htm

Developing and transition countries – latest research

There has been more recent work on the size and development of the informal economy labour force in developing and transition countries.[8] For example, Kucera and Roncolato (2008: 321) deal with informal employment. They address issues of crucial importance to labour market policy. Informal employment in developing countries can be 'voluntary' in the same sense that it is voluntary in developed countries. In such cases, individuals

8   See also Feld and Schneider (2010), Schneider et al. (2010), Williams (2010a, 2010b, 2011a, 2011b) and Hazans (2011).

Table 18 **Share of informal employment in total non-agricultural employment**

Region	Average share of informal employment in total non-agricultural employment			
	1985–89	1990–94	1995–99	2000–07
22 South and Middle American countries	32.4	35.4	40.3	50.1
34 Asian countries	55.9	60.4	65.4	70.2
42 African countries	40.3	47.1	52.4	60.5
21 transition countries	30.9	32.3	35.4	40.2

Sources: OECD (2009a: 34–5) and Charmes (2000); for the ILO, Women and Men in the Informal Economy, 2002; for the most recent period, Heintz and Chang (2007) for the ILO

who have opportunities in formal labour markets may choose to work in the informal economy to avoid social security contributions and so on. Others, however, may work informally because of the difficulties – especially perhaps in rural areas – of formalising employment relationships and registering businesses. The authors conclude that certain forms of labour market regulation cause informal employment, but do not suggest that all moves to reduce labour market regulation are necessarily beneficial.

Table 18 shows the share of informal employment in total non-agricultural employment by region. The share of informal employment has increased over time. For example, the share of informal employment in South and Central American countries in the period 1985–89 was 32.4 per cent, and this had increased by the period 2000–07 to 50.1 per cent. There were similar increases in Asia and Africa. It should be noted that these figures use total informal employment as the numerator (agricultural and non-agricultural) but only non-agricultural employment in

Table 19 **Informal employment as a proportion of non-agricultural employment, by country, region and gender, 1990s and 2000s**

Region	1990–99 % (averages unweighted for countries for which data are available). Blank cells indicate no data available		2000–07 % (averages unweighted for countries for which data are available). Blank cells indicate no data available	
	Women	Men	Women	Men
North Africa	43.3	49.3	38.6	47.2
Algeria	40.6	43.1		
Morocco	46.8	44.0		
Tunisia	39.2	53.2		
Egypt	46.5	56.9	38.6	47.2
Sub-Saharan Africa	84.1	63.0	77.1	62.6
Benin	97.3	87.0		
Chad	95.2	59.5		
Guinea	86.7	65.6		
Kenya	83.1	59.1		
Mali			89.2	74.2
South Africa	58.4	43.6	64.9	51.0
Latin America	56.2	47.1	59.5	55.4
Bolivia	74.4	55.0		
Brazil	67.3	54.7	52.3	50.2
Chile	43.9	30.9		
Colombia	44.0	34.1		
Costa Rica	48.0	42.1		
Dominican Republic	49.7	46.5		
Ecuador			76.9	73.2
El Salvador	68.6	45.7		
Guatemala	69.4	46.5		
Honduras	65.5	73.6		
Mexico	55.0	54.3	53.5	47.8
Panama	40.8	35.5	50.4	48.7
Peru			72.0	65.1

Region	1990–99 % (averages unweighted for countries for which data are available). Blank cells indicate no data available		2000–07 % (averages unweighted for countries for which data are available). Blank cells indicate no data available	
	Women	Men	Women	Men
Venezuela	47.3	46.7	52.1	47.5
South and South-East Asia	72.7	70.2		
India	85.7	82.9		
Indonesia	77.2	78.0		
Philippines	73.4	70.8		
Thailand	54.3	49.1		
West Asia	31.1	43.4	35.4	44.4
Lebanon			60.0	44.4
West Bank and Gaza Strip			20.2	46.8
Syria	34.6	42.8		
Turkey	19.1	29.1	32.2	33.4
Yemen	39.7	58.2	29.3	52.8
Transition countries			22.3	27.2
Kyrgyzstan			40.9	47.1
Moldova			18.4	28.0
Russia			7.6	9.6

Source: OECD (2009a: 47) and Charmes (2000); for the ILO, Women and Men in the Informal Economy, 2002; for the most recent period, Heintz and Chang (2007) for the ILO and for West Asia

the denominator, and thus the informal economy workforce as a proportion of the total workforce is smaller than the figures shown.

Table 19 shows the proportion of informal employment in total non-agricultural employment by country, region and gender. The proportion of women in the informal economy in some regions is significantly higher than the proportion of men.

In sub-Saharan Africa, for example, the proportion of women in the informal labour market is 84 per cent and that of men is 63 per cent. In general the proportion of informal employment is high worldwide in transition and developing countries. As noted, this is partly because of the limited ability of many businesses and individuals to formalise employment relationships so that informal employment essentially becomes the norm.

Disaggregating shadow employment – some further investigation

It has already been noted that the forms which shadow employment takes will be different in different countries. In some countries, self-employment is not discouraged and has a separate tax status, whereas in other countries self-employment can involve shadow arrangements without clear contracts for service. The self-employed will often not pay the same rates of social insurance contributions as those who are employed but, at the same time, they may not receive the relevant benefits either. The situation of those undertaking shadow employment for a few hours a week while also having a full-time job is very different from that of those who work full time in the shadow economy. It is possible to understand more about the nature of the shadow economy and the policies that can be used to address it by looking at particular features of shadow work.

The proportion of employees not covered by social security contributions

There is highly likely to be a relationship between state-provided social security and the shadow economy. Those who work in the shadow economy may well generally do so in order to avoid paying taxes – including social security taxes. In contributory systems where benefits are closely related to a contribution record, however, such people will also not receive benefits, although they may still receive low levels of subsistence support from the state during old age or periods of unemployment.

The extent of social security contributions in a number of OECD countries can be seen in Table 20. The very high tax wedge will undoubtedly contribute to encouraging the shadow economy, and there certainly appears to be some relationship between the level of social security taxes and the size of the shadow economy, something which is, of course, confirmed in the formal studies discussed in earlier chapters.

Table 20 **Social insurance contributions wedge for a selection of countries**

Country	Social security contributions from employers and employees, % of salary
Germany	40
Italy	41
Portugal	34
Switzerland	12
United Kingdom	26

Notes: Contributions vary according to salary: these are the marginal rates around the middle of the salary range as it is marginal rates which affect shadow economy decisions. Rates are approximate from OECD data. Arguably, rates should be expressed as a percentage of the employee's value added, which would involve adding back the employer's contribution to the salary, and this would reduce rates where the employer's contribution is large. For example, in the case of Germany, the rate would fall to 33 per cent if calculated as a percentage of salary plus employer's contribution.

Table 21 **Proportion of employees not covered by social security contributions**

	Proportion of non-insured employees	
	2007	2008
Austria	35.4	34.5
Belgium	38.8	36.2
Czech Republic	40.8	40.4
Estonia	34.6	33.9
Finland	23.0	23.5
France	51.9	–
Greece	37.1	37.3
Hungary	40.6	42.4
Iceland	13.4	13.3
Ireland	39.8	40.3
Italy	40.0	39.3
Luxembourg	34.6	32.6
Netherlands	17.7	21.6
Norway	12.2	13.2
Poland	65.3	57.0
Portugal	35.1	38.5
Slovak Republic	39.1	38.5
Slovenia	24.7	25.2
Spain	41.5	41.4
Sweden	22.7	22.0

Source: OECD calculation based on EU-SILC 2007 and 2008, quoted in OECD (2011: 18, Table 1)

It does not follow that all those who are not paying social security contributions are working in the shadow economy. There are likely to be at least four categories of individuals who are not paying social security contributions: those who are evading contributions; those who work in sectors where contributions are not required and formal employment arrangements are not compulsory (for example, in agriculture in many countries); those whose earnings are insufficient to require them to pay contributions; and those who are self-employed and neither make contributions nor receive benefits.

Table 21 shows the proportion of employees not paying social security contributions for a selection of European Union countries. In some countries, this share is very high. The highest level is in Poland, with well over 50 per cent of the workforce not paying contributions, followed by France and Spain. It is highly likely that many of these workers are operating in the shadow economy.

Strengthening the contributory principle within social security systems – or privatisation – is likely to reduce the size of the shadow economy. Individuals who undertake shadow work will then lose social security entitlements as well as avoiding taxes. The contributory principle can be strengthened by ensuring that pensions are closely linked to the number of years worked; by ensuring that unconditional unemployment and sickness payments are provided only to people with a contribution record; and by ensuring that contributions match benefit scales (either by having flat-rate contributions for flat-rate benefits or earnings-related contributions for earnings-related benefits).[9] Privatisation can be facilitated by allowing people to 'opt out' of social security systems and make their own private arrangements.

---

9   The UK is an example of a country where there are very few advantages from making social security (national insurance) contributions as benefits are not related to contributions in most parts of the system. Employers and employees between them can save about 23 per cent of the gross wage by avoiding social security contributions with very little loss to benefits.

Table 22 **Alternative measures of informal employment and undeclared work, 2006 (percentage of non-farm employment)**

Country	Employees in informal jobs		Own-account workers	Unpaid family workers	Multiple job holders	Undeclared income	
	Employees not registered for mandatory social security	Employees without work contract				% of work-force typically not re-ported for tax purposes	% of employees receiving wages cash in hand
Czech Republic	–	1.8	11.4	0.7	2.1	10.1	3.0
Hungary	19.4	2.6	6.4	0.3	1.8	8.6	8.0
Korea	25.8	–	17.1	4.7	1.7	7.0	–
Mexico	31.5	26.9	20.6	5.1	3.3	30.9	–
Poland	–	4.9	7.0	0.7	7.5	10.6	11.0
Slovak Republic	–	2.2	9.2	0.1	1.2	5.6	7.0
Turkey	21.7	–	16.6	3.3	3.1	24.6	–

Source: OECD (2008, 2011: 20, Table 3.1)

Types of informal employment

As has been noted, there are a variety of ways in which shadow economy work can take place. This can include individuals not being registered for social security contributions to avoid contributions; individuals who work without a contract; those who have second jobs and declare only one of those jobs; illegal immigrants who cannot legally register; and those who work casually and occasionally for cash in hand.

An OECD study (2008) examines the different forms of informal employment in seven OECD countries: the Czech Republic, Hungary, Korea, Mexico, Poland, the Slovak Republic and Turkey. The results are shown in Table 22. Informal workers are grouped by informal job and own-account workers; unpaid family workers; multiple job holders; and those with undeclared income. Mexico has the highest values for almost all of these seven categories, followed by Turkey and then Korea. There are large variations in the forms of informal working between the countries. For example, former communist countries have a very low proportion of unpaid family workers but a fairly high proportion of multiple job holders compared with other forms of informal employment.

Shadow economy workers with an illegal immigrant background

The OECD has collected data about illegal immigrants who are working in the shadow economy and this is summarised in Figure 5. These numbers are small but significant. They are particularly important because, in many cases, illegal immigrants may well have full-time jobs in the shadow economy. The highest level of illegal migrant working is in Greece (4.4 per cent), followed by the USA (3.2 per cent) and Italy (2 per cent). Norway and Sweden have the lowest values.

It is worth noting, however, that the employment of illegal immigrants takes place at relatively small levels in all the countries below. Indeed, given the situation that illegal immigrants find themselves in, one can view shadow working by this group rather positively in that the alternative might be relying on charity

Figure 5   Illegal employed immigrants as a share of total employment

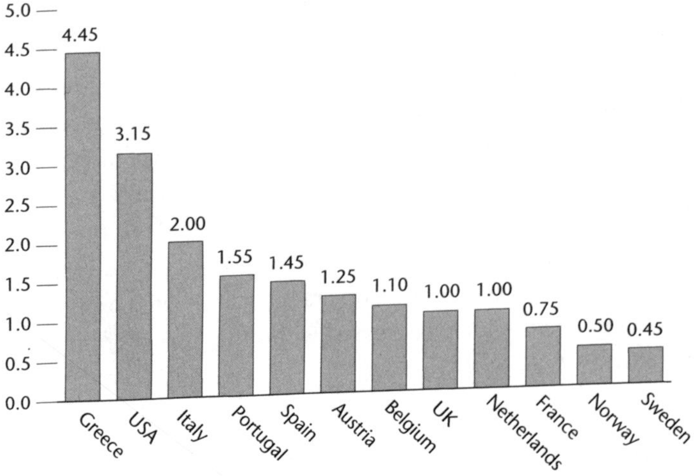

Notes: The estimates of the number of employed illegal immigrants are calculated using the number of irregular migrants and assuming the same employment rate for illegal immigrants as for legal migrants.
Source: OECD Calculations based on *OECD International Migration Outlook* (2009) and OECD Economic Outlook Database (2010), quoted from OECD (2011), p. 21, Figure 10.

or begging. Policies to address the problem (on the one hand amnesties and, on the other hand, either strengthening border policing or liberalising immigration policy) would clearly make a discernible impact on this group but, in the context of the shadow economy as a whole, illegal immigration is not the most important issue.

6 THE SHADOW ECONOMY AND UNEMPLOYMENT[1]

Theoretical relationships between the shadow economy and unemployment

Although there has been some work to attempt to quantify the size of the shadow economy labour force and its causes, comparatively little attention has been given to the relationship between unemployment and working in the shadow economy. As Tanzi (1999) points out: 'the current literature does not cast much light on these relationships even though the existence of large underground activities would imply that one should look more deeply at what is happening in the labour market' (p. 347).

Bajada and Schneider (2009) examine the extent of participation in the shadow economy by the unemployed and investigate the relationship between the unemployment rate and the shadow economy. It is possible that those involved in the shadow economy are recorded as unemployed and therefore that true rates of unemployment are overstated. The literature on this topic has suggested, however, that the relationship between the shadow economy and unemployment is ambiguous. This is because those working in the shadow economy form a heterogeneous group of people – some will have other jobs; some will work in the shadow

---

1   Much of the first part of Chapter 6 is taken from Feld and Schneider (2010).

economy only for a few hours a week while claiming unemployment benefits; others may claim benefits while working many hours in the shadow economy; and so on. There are also various cyclical forces at work. Overall, the net effect is that the shadow economy is weakly correlated with unemployment.

A model has been proposed by Bajada and Schneider for disentangling these effects. We can think of a 'substitution effect' which involves shadow economy work increasing with unemployment in the sense that shadow economy work acts as a substitute for the lack of formal employment available. The extent of this effect can be found by examining cyclical variations in unemployment. The model suggests that shadow economy work does typically increase during periods of declining legitimate economic activity (and therefore increasing unemployment) as shadow economy work replaces work in the formal economy. The relationship tends to be symmetrical in that, as unemployment increases, shadow work increases and, as unemployment decreases, shadow work also decreases. Indeed, as well as being similar in terms of sign, the relationships are also similar in terms of their magnitude for both increases and decreases in unemployment. It would appear, therefore, that the shadow economy acts as a source of financial support during periods of cyclical unemployment for those genuinely wanting to participate in the legitimate economy, although this does not exclude the possibility that long-term unemployed may also be participating in the shadow economy and that those with jobs may constitute the majority of those working in the shadow economy, even if the participation rate is higher among the unemployed.

We might also expect unemployment support programmes to affect shadow economic work. The analysis of various unemployment support programmes across twelve OECD countries, however, does not appear to produce a strong systematic relationship between the generosity of social security systems and the nature of short-term shadow economic activity by the unemployed. Even the various benefit replacement rates across OECD countries appear to have little effect on the rate at which the unemployed take on or cut back shadow economy activity. Again, there are several potential effects that may be difficult to disentangle. A high replacement rate may make it less likely that somebody who is unemployed will take on shadow work to supplement their income. It may make it more likely, however, that they will remain unemployed and therefore in a position to supplement their benefit income illegally. Furthermore, ways in which the unemployment programmes are managed will also affect the tendency for individuals to take on shadow work.

On the whole Bajada and Schneider argue that dealing with the participation of the unemployed in the shadow economy is best handled by more stringent monitoring of those receiving unemployment benefits to reintegrate them into the workforce rather than by reducing benefit replacement rates. It is possible that a strategy of reducing replacement rates would lead to there being inadequate support for those experiencing financial hardship during periods of unemployment while having little impact on reducing participation by the unemployed who are willing and able to engage in shadow economy activity. This does, of course, depend on the pre-existing level of benefits. Perhaps the main lesson of the limited literature in this field, however, is that benefit levels should be determined by criteria other than their possible impact on the size of the shadow economy.

The shadow economy and unemployment in the European Union

Further work has been undertaken by Williams and Nadin (2012), who analyse groups of EU countries in greater detail using the results of the 2007 Eurobarometer survey. Specifically, they examine the idea that the unemployed disproportionately participate in, and gain from, undeclared work (the 'marginalisation' thesis) and the 'reinforcement' thesis, which holds that the unemployed benefit less from undeclared work than those in declared employment, meaning that undeclared work reinforces, rather than reduces, the inequalities produced by the formal economy. Which of these explanations is valid is potentially an important policy issue. These two phenomena are not entirely mutually exclusive.

Table 23 contains data which allows us to evaluate which of these theses is valid in different parts of the EU-27. In Nordic nations, only 9 per cent of the unemployed participate in undeclared work compared with 12 per cent of the employed and 20 per cent of other non-employed. The result is that, although the unemployed constitute 4 per cent of the surveyed population, they conduct just 3 per cent of all undeclared work and receive just 2 per cent of all undeclared income. Indeed, the employed receive considerably higher pay per hour from shadow work than the unemployed. This suggests that the reinforcement thesis is more important in these countries.

The marginalisation thesis would appear to be valid, however – at least to some extent – in western Europe, east-central Europe and southern Europe. In western Europe, 6 per cent of the unemployed conduct undeclared work compared with 5 per cent of the employed and 4 per cent of other non-employed. In east-central

Table 23 **Extent and nature of participation of employed, unemployed and non-employed in undeclared work, by EU region**

	% engaging in undeclared work	% of all undeclared work conducted by:	% of surveyed population	Average total hours	Average hourly undeclared wage (€)	Mean annual undeclared income/ undeclared worker (€)	% of total undeclared income in EU-27 earned by:
EU-27	4	100	100	80	11.02	881	*100*
Unemployed	9	11	6	98	8.04	788	9
Other non-employed	3	32	44	81	9.31	754	30
All employed	5	57	50	77	14.08	1084	61
Nordic nations	11	100	100	40	13.75	550	*100*
Unemployed	9	3	4	42	11.83	497	*2*
Other non-employed	20	34	39	43	11.81	508	32
All employed	12	63	57	37	15.20	562	66
Western Europe	4	100	100	58	12.82	744	*100*
Unemployed	6	8	6	52	9.94	517	5
Other non-employed	4	35	43	65	10.38	674	32
All employed	5	57	51	59	14.90	879	63
East-Central Europe	5	100	100	98	7.34	720	*100*
Unemployed	12	17	7	136	5.24	713	17
Other non-employed	3	21	45	85	6.20	527	16
All employed	7	62	48	96	8.31	798	67
Southern Europe	3	100	100	120	9.14	1096	*100*
Unemployed	12	16	4	141	8.98	1266	18
Other non-employed	2	40	46	138	7.88	1087	39
All employed	2	44	50	111	10.30	1143	43

Source: Williams and Nadin (2012)

Europe 12 per cent of the unemployed conduct undeclared work but just 7 per cent of the employed and 3 per cent of other non-employed. In southern Europe, 12 per cent of the unemployed conducted undeclared work in the last twelve months but just 2 per cent of the employed and 2 per cent of the other non-employed.

In western Europe and east-central Europe, the reinforcement thesis is valid too. The employed undertake more shadow work and also benefit more from it in terms of pay. This means that shadow work reinforces existing recorded patterns of inequality. In western Europe, despite constituting only 51 per cent of the surveyed population, the employed conduct 57 per cent of shadow work and earn 63 per cent of all undeclared income at a rate of 50 per cent more per hour than the unemployed. Similarly, in east-central Europe, despite constituting only 48 per cent of the surveyed population, the employed conduct 62 per cent of undeclared work, earn 67 per cent of the total undeclared income and earn 59 per cent more per hour than unemployed undertaking shadow work.

In southern Europe, however, it would appear that only the marginalisation thesis applies. Despite constituting 50 per cent of the surveyed population, the employed conduct just 44 per cent of undeclared work and earn just 43 per cent of the undeclared income.

Policy implications

This evidence has important policy implications. It should be noted first that these patterns might well reflect existing policy. For example, Nordic countries tend to have reasonably well-functioning labour markets and also relatively strong requirements to look for and take work that is available. They also have high levels of benefit payments through unemployment insurance schemes that are often private (though partly state-funded). A combination of strong work requirements and a relatively high level of insurance-based benefits would seem to provide the right incentives to reduce shadow economy work among the unemployed. At the same time, high marginal tax rates may well encourage shadow economy work among the employed.

In western and east-central Europe, undeclared work would seem to reinforce the marginalisation of the unemployed given the low levels of remuneration the unemployed obtain from shadow work. At the same time, shadow work is prevalent among the unemployed. It would seem clear that some combination of targeting the unemployed with appropriate detection and deterrence measures and developing social insurance systems that provide incentives and assistance to return to work in the formal economy should be a priority. Such approaches can also be effective in reducing welfare fraud, including among people who have a job in the regular economy while claiming benefits.

In addition, it is important that impediments to formal employment and the registering of self-employed businesses are reduced. These issues will be discussed further below. These policy implications would appear to be particularly relevant to southern European countries given the high levels of shadow work undertaken by all the non-employed (including those who are not claiming welfare benefits).

7 TACKLING THE SHADOW ECONOMY – AN OVERVIEW

The earlier chapters have shown how large the shadow economy is, even in developed countries with reasonably effective rule of law and tax collection systems. It has also been shown how there could be a vicious circle of higher government spending, higher taxes, more shadow economy work, less tax revenue collected, higher tax rates, more shadow economy work, lower tax morale, and so on ... The features of the shadow economy are different in different countries and, in particular, the role that the unemployed play in the shadow economy, relative to those who are employed, varies from country to country. This means that the appropriate response can vary. In some countries it may be more appropriate to focus on the benefits systems, in others on businesses employing people, and elsewhere on the self-employed. Nevertheless, there are some general measures that can be expected to reduce the size of the shadow economy – at least to some extent – in a wide range of situations. In the remaining chapters of this monograph we examine and evaluate measures that could be used to reduce the size of the shadow economy.

We explicitly exclude, in these later chapters, 'meta measures' such as reducing the size of government spending and the tax burden significantly. While the work of the earlier chapters suggests that this could be a very important approach, there are policy implications of taking that approach which go well beyond the scope of this monograph. Suffice to say that, if a country is considering reducing government spending significantly, for other reasons, a potential reduction in the shadow economy is a possible relevant side effect. In these later chapters, we also focus on the shadow economy in generally higher-income countries and not the informal economy in less developed countries. In the latter case, simple approaches to ensure that contracts are recognised and enforced, property rights promoted and registered and that business activity can be easily registered can be especially important (see De Soto, 2000).

The remainder of this chapter introduces three broad policy options for dealing with the shadow economy: doing nothing; eradication; and legitimising the shadow economy. Doing nothing leaves intact the existing negative impacts on legitimate and shadow businesses, as well as on customers and governments. Eradicating the shadow economy stamps out precisely the entre-preneurship and enterprise culture that governments wish to nurture. This means that, though some deterrence measures are appropriate, only legitimising the shadow economy by enabling its formalisation is likely to be widely successful. The following chapters then review a range of policy measures used in different countries to legitimise the shadow economy. The result is a plethora of policies that might be used individually or in combination to help transfer work currently in the shadow economy into the legitimate realm.

Tackling the shadow economy: broad policy approaches

Do nothing

A first potential policy option is to 'do nothing' about the shadow economy. The rationale is that over half of all businesses start up operating in the shadow economy and that this sphere is therefore a principal seedbed for new enterprise creation, a breeding ground for the micro-enterprise system and a test bed for fledgling businesses (Williams, 2006) and should therefore be left alone. The problem, however, is that this hidden enterprise culture has negative impacts on legitimate businesses, those working in the shadow economy, their customers and governments.

Legitimate businesses witness unfair competition from such enterprises, meaning that they end up paying higher taxes than would otherwise be the case and cannot compete on a level playing field with them (Evans et al., 2006; Renooy et al., 2004; Gallin, 2001; Grabiner, 2000; Williams and Windebank, 1998). Even if the reality is that their tax burden does not rise significantly as a result of shadow entrepreneurs, the affect on tax morale can be damaging. The tax system could come to be perceived as unfair.

At the same time, shadow entrepreneurs are unable to develop and grow owing to their inability to gain access to capital, advertise their business or secure support (Evans et al., 2006; Gallin, 2001; ILO, 2002). This is a particular problem in less developed countries. Customers of shadow enterprises, furthermore, find themselves without legal recourse if a poor job is done; without insurance cover; without guarantees in relation to the work conducted; and with no certainty that health and safety regulations have been followed. Those working for the shadow economy business encounter similar problems. Finally, governments witness a loss of revenue in terms of non-payment of taxes owed and, if a significant segment routinely engage in such endeavour, it may well encourage a more casual attitude towards the law more widely (Renooy et al., 2004; Williams, 2006). In sum, the negative impacts of doing nothing mean that actions to tackle the shadow economy are desirable.

Eradicating the shadow economy

A second option is to stamp out the shadow economy. If we treat the shadow labour force as rational economic actors who evade tax because the pay-off is greater than the expected cost of being caught and punished (Allingham and Sandmo, 1972), the cost–benefit ratio confronting those engaged in – or considering engaging in – shadow work could be changed by increasing the costs in the form of the perceived or actual likelihood of detection and the penalties and sanctions for those caught (e.g. Grabiner, 2000; Richardson and Sawyer, 2001).

The major problem with such an eradication approach is that the shadow economy is a principal breeding ground and seed bed for entrepreneurship, so eradicating it will stamp out precisely the entrepreneurship and enterprise culture that is needed for economic development and growth (Small Business Council, 2004; Williams, 2006).

Legitimising the shadow economy

A third policy option is to facilitate the legitimisation of work in the shadow economy (European Commission, 2007; Dekker et al. 2010; Renooy et al., 2004; Small Business Council, 2004;

Williams, 2006; Williams and Renooy, 2009). How might this be achieved?

On the one hand, a 'push' approach can be adopted. Deterrence measures can be pursued to change the cost–benefit ratio confronting those thinking about working in the shadow economy by changing the cost side of the equation through improving the perceived or actual likelihood of detection and increasing the fines and sanctions for those caught. The aim here is not to stamp out the shadow economic activity but to provide incentives for it to be brought within the legal economy. On its own, however, such a 'push' approach might well simply eradicate the enterprise and entrepreneurship, thus bringing with it the disadvantages of the eradication approach.

A 'pull' approach could be used instead. Here, more enabling measures are adopted that make participating in the official economy easier and more beneficial. These enabling measures are of three kinds. Firstly, preventive measures can be pursued to deter new entrants into the shadow economy. Secondly, curative measures can be pursued to help those already participating in the shadow economy to transfer into the official realm. Thirdly and finally, commitment measures can be adopted that seek to encourage an allegiance to tax morality (Alm et al., 1995; Andreoni et al., 1998; Cullis and Lewis, 1997; Smith and Kinsey, 1987; Torgler, 2003; Weigel et al., 1987; Wenzel, 2002). These approaches and the accompanying measures that might be used are summarised in Table 24.

These various policy measures that can be pursued to legitimise the shadow economy are of course not mutually exclusive. A government, for example, might simplify regulatory compliance and, at the same time, introduce incentives to enter the legitimate

Table 24 **Policy measures for legitimising the shadow economy**

Approach	Method	Measures (examples)
Deterrence (pursue and punish)	Improved detection	Data matching and sharing Joined up strategy Joint operations
	Increased penalties	Increased penalties for evasion
	Increase perception of risk	Advertising the penalties for informal working Advertising the effectiveness of detection procedures
Enabling formalisation	Prevention (deter entry)	Simplification of compliance Direct and indirect tax incentives Smooth transition to self-employment Introducing new categories of work Micro-enterprise development
	Curative (encourage movement out of shadow economy)	Demand-side incentives (e.g. service vouchers; targeted direct taxes; targeted indirect taxes) Supply-side incentives (e.g. society-wide amnesties; voluntary disclosure; formalisation services)
	Fostering commitment (retain in the formal economy)	Promoting benefits of formal work Education Peer-to-peer surveillance Tax fairness Procedural justice Redistributive justice

realm (such as amnesties) and then, for those who fail to comply, implement tougher sanctions for those subsequently caught. At the same time campaigns might be introduced to elicit greater commitment to tax morality. Various approaches to legitimising the shadow economy are discussed in the remaining chapters.

8 TACKLING THE SHADOW ECONOMY THROUGH DETERRENCE MEASURES

Improved detection

As noted above, deterrence measures can involve increasing penalties or increasing the likelihood of being caught. Measures to improve the perceived or actual likelihood of detection focus on two issues: increasing the effectiveness of inspections, and joining up strategy and operations, including data matching and sharing, either at the national or cross-national level.

Nearly all tax authorities pursue initiatives to improve the effectiveness of inspections. These initiatives range from increasing the number of inspections through to improving the effectiveness of inspections in terms of, for example, the number of instances of shadow work identified and the value of the undeclared tax collected or sanctions imposed. To achieve this, administrations have, for instance, concentrated inspections on 'suspect' sectors where shadow work is rife. 'Announced inspection visits' have also been used, whereby a place and/or sector is informed that a visit is to occur in the near future. This has been done in sectors such as hotels and restaurants in countries such as Denmark. The pre-announcement of the visit can be expected to lead to a reduction in tax evasion without penalties being imposed.

Two other common approaches to improve the effectiveness

of inspections have been to ensure that workers are registered prior to commencing work and the use of identity cards. In the past, it was commonly the case that, when an inspector visited a workplace, the owner would claim that the worker had just started that day and therefore had not yet been registered. To overcome this, many countries have now introduced the compulsory registration of workers before they start work. In nations such as Germany and Austria, moreover, customers (whether businesses or households) have been made liable for any instances of shadow work identified (see Williams and Renooy, 2009). These approaches are not without their disadvantages – for example, they may raise costs on businesses.

Identity cards may or may not work as a deterrent but they are a potential tool to facilitate detection of unregistered workers. Between August 2006 and December 2007 in Italy, the inspections of 37,129 construction sites revealed that 57 per cent of firms were irregular and that 63 per cent of workers regularly employed on construction sites were unregistered (Ministero del Lavoro, della Salute e delle Politiche Sociali, 2008).

Identity cards have also been implemented voluntarily by the business sector in a bid to clean up their sector and stifle the shadow economy. In Sweden, for instance, the construction industry has implemented its own voluntary registration scheme, namely ID06, as described in the box.

The use of industry registration schemes, of course, circumvents the wider objections to and problems that might arise with government identity card systems.

To improve detection, another popular initiative is to enhance the coordination of strategy and operations, including data sharing. On the one hand, this has occurred on a national level, as

ID06 project, Sweden

The construction industry in Sweden has introduced a voluntarily system of staff registration using identity cards, namely the ID06 project initiated in 2007 by a group of organisations within the construction sector called 'The Construction Sector in Co-operation' (translated from Byggbranschen i Samverkan, BiS). The members are seven business organisations and five trade unions within the construction sector. The head organisation is the Swedish Construction Federation (Sveriges Byggindustrier, BI).
The ID06 project consists of the following measures:

- A requirement that everyone who attends a construction site must carry valid ID06 identification.
- The subcontractor is obliged to register the employees in advance with the head contractor.
- Daily registration of authorised employees at the workplace.
- The daily registration must be saved for two years and be available at the site in case of a control visit from the National Tax Agency.
- The head contractor has the right to remove anyone from the construction site who is not authorised.
- The head contractor has the right to demand a fine of 500 SEK (€50) per person per day if employees cannot show the required identification.

Some three hundred card readers and 60,000 identity cards have been distributed, with 8,000 new identity cards issued each month. About two thousand companies, including all major national ones, are now involved in ID06. The ID06 card costs 90 SEK (€9) per employee. The card reader device costs 8,000 SEK (€800).

exemplified by Belgium. On the other hand, there have also been limited attempts to achieve cross-national cooperation on data sharing, such as on the ownership of foreign bank accounts.

Despite the widespread advocacy of measures to improve detection, evaluations are far from conclusive as to whether such measures have proved effective. Some studies find that increasing the probability of detection reduces participation in shadow work for some income groups at least (Beron et al., 1992; Dubin and Wilde, 1988; Dubin et al., 1987; Slemrod et al., 2001). Others find, however, that it actually leads to a growth in shadow work and/ or has little or no effect on overall compliance levels (Bergman and Nevarez, 2006; Elffers et al., 1987; Friedland, 1982; Kornhauser, 2008; Murphy, 2008; Spicer and Lunstedt, 1976; Varma and Doob, 1998; Webley and Halstead, 1986). Instead, it is often argued that the level of voluntary compliance is in only small part explained by the existence of effective audit, inspection and detection regimes. In major part, such compliance is explained by the degree to which there is a commitment to tax morality in the population (Kornhauser, 2008; Murphy, 2008). For these reasons, a cautious approach is urged regarding the improvement of detection as anything other than a contributory measure for tackling the shadow economy.

Increased penalties

Given the high costs involved in increasing the probability of detection, it is sometimes decided to impose higher penalties for participating in the shadow economy. The evidence is again by no means clear-cut, however, that this is an effective way of legitimising or reducing the shadow economy. While some studies find that increasing fines reduces the shadow economy (De Juan et al., 1994; Friedland et al., 1978; Klepper and Nagin, 1989; Schwartz and Orleans, 1967), others conclude that increasing penalties leads to a growth in such work and/or has no effect, or only a short-term effect, on compliance (Chang and Lai, 2004; Elffers et al., 1987; Feld and Frey, 2002a; Friedland, 1982; Murphy, 2005, 2008; Spicer and Lunstedt, 1976; Varma and Doob, 1998; Webley and Halstead, 1986; Williams, 2001). This is because imposing penalties can be counterproductive and undermine the relationship between the legal authorities and those they seek to regulate (Ayres and Braithwaite, 1992; Blumenthal et al., 1998). The use of threat and legal coercion can lead to the opposite behaviour from that sought. Increasing the penalties can result in greater non-compliance (Murphy and Harris, 2007), creative compliance (McBarnet, 2003), criminal behaviour or overt opposition (Fehr and Rokenbach, 2003; Frey, 1997a; Kagan and Scholz, 1984). In other words, it can increase resistance to compliance.

In consequence, increasing penalties has unintended impacts. One principal reason for raising penalties is to increase the amount of tax revenue to be collected. A Danish study found, however, that the purchasers of shadow work would prefer to resort to do-it-yourself activities (34 per cent) or simply not consume the services (30 per cent) rather than pay the official formal price (Mogensen, 1985). Hence, nearly two-thirds of shadow work would not be converted into declared jobs this way and, instead, the work would simply not take place.

Another potential unintended impact of increasing penalties (and detection) is that it may cause a reduction in tax morale and therefore an unintended growth in the shadow economy. For instance, an analysis of the 1987 American Taxpayer Opinion

Survey (Smith, 1992) reveals that perceived procedural fairness and responsiveness in providing a service were positive incentives that increased taxpayers' commitment to paying taxes. Meanwhile, Kinsey (1992) found that, while detection and punishments are used to attempt to force people to comply, these processes also alienate taxpayers and reduce voluntary compliance. An increase in the perceived severity of punishment and likelihood of detection may therefore amplify rather than lower tax evasion by reducing respect for the system's fairness. This is also confirmed by the findings of Murphy (2005, 2008).

Indeed, Wenzel (2004a), in a survey of 1,406 Australian citizens, finds that increasing penalties works only where individual ethics are weak. Where social norms are strongly in favour of tax honesty, increasing severity of sanctions increases tax evasion. Harsh penalties and tax morality, therefore, are not comfortable bedfellows. This does not mean, however, that they cannot be used in a temporal sequence. For example, Davis et al. (2003) find that harsh enforcement increases compliance among previously non-compliant taxpayers and that returning to the previous more lax system does not necessarily cause them to return to their previous behaviour. This suggests that harsh penalties followed by their reduction and a shift towards more enabling measures could be an effective means of eliciting ongoing compliance since those who were previously outside would be then within the compliance system. For those already compliant, however, such a regime would perhaps have the perverse effect of increasing their non-compliance.

A final but important finding regarding the effectiveness of deterrence is that many participants in the shadow economy are not rational economic actors swayed by the cost–benefit ratios confronting them. As the 2007 Eurobarometer survey reveals, the greater part (55 per cent) of shadow work is conducted for and by kin, neighbours, friends and acquaintances, and such work is often conducted for redistributive reasons rather than purely financial gain. This has important implications for tackling the shadow economy. It can no longer be assumed that all participants are rational economic actors seeking to make or save money and that therefore shadow work can be tackled simply by changing the cost–benefit ratio confronting them.

To summarise, the evidence that improving detection and increasing penalties improves compliance is less than conclusive. Not surprisingly, therefore, other approaches and measures are beginning to be used beyond 'push' factors to try to legitimise the shadow economy and help move shadow work into the official economy.

9 TACKLING THE SHADOW ECONOMY BY ENABLING FORMALISATION

Deterring entry

To discourage entry into the shadow economy, a number of broad policy measures can be adopted.

Simplifying regulatory compliance

Legal and administrative requirements, such as registration and licensing, can pose an obstacle to small companies declaring work. Compliance costs per worker are often much higher for small companies because of the economies of scale involved in dealing with regulation (see Chittenden et al., 2002, 2003; Hansford et al., 2003; Hart et al., 2005; Michaelis et al., 2001; OECD, 2000). Where the costs of administrative compliance are prohibitive, compliance is often low (see Adams and Webley, 2001; ILO, 2002; Matthews and Lloyd-Williams, 2001). Examples of administrative costs associated with regulatory compliance include the filling out of forms, the payment of tax, inspection (rather than advice), inconsistent application of the rules by different regulators or even different inspectors within the same regulator, and duplication of information requirements from different regulators. Indeed, in an analysis of 45 countries, Richardson (2006) shows that complexity is the most significant determinant of non-compliance, followed

'On the Spot' firm (*Empresa na Hora*), Portugal

In 2005, the Ministry of Justice announced the Simplex programme for administrative and legislative simplification. The 'On the Spot' firm is one initiative under this Simplex programme, which seeks to alleviate the processes and procedures necessary to set up a new firm. This initiative makes it possible to create a company in a single office (one-stop shop) and in a single day. Upon completion, the definitive legal person identification card is handed over, the social security number given and the company immediately receives its memorandum and articles of association and an extract of the entry in the Commercial Register. The security of the incorporation procedure for new enterprises is ensured by having all the details sent to the tax authorities.

Between 2005, when the initiative started, and September 2008, 59,068 new enterprises were created: 574 public limited companies (1 per cent of the total), 34,934 private limited companies (59 per cent) and 23,560 one-person companies (40 per cent). The average time taken is one hour and fourteen minutes and the average cost of setting up a company is €360. Whether such administrative simplification has reduced the shadow economy has not been directly evaluated.

Many countries are investigating the transferability of this initiative. After being recognised as a success by the World Bank, Angola and Cape Verde, for example, have already asked for legal and technical support, and countries such as Slovenia, Hungary, Egypt, Mozambique, Chile, Brazil, Finland, Sweden and China have visited the 'On the Spot' firm service to understand how Portugal has managed to simplify the procedures required for establishing a new firm.

by education, income source, fairness and tax morale. Overall, Richardson's regression results show that the lower the level of complexity – and the higher the level of education, fairness and tax morale – the lower the level of tax non-compliance.

Thus, a potential way forward is to reduce the costs and complexity of regulatory compliance. One option to deter entry into the shadow economy is to simplify the procedures and lower the costs of establishing and operating a small business – for instance, through easier registration procedures and reasonable and fair taxation, as shown in the box.

Simplifying regulatory compliance, however, need not solely involve relatively minor administrative changes. Measures could also include more fundamental overhauls of the tax system, such as introducing a standard deduction for the expenses of self-employed people on their tax returns (Elffers and Hessing, 1997). In any sector or occupation, a tax authority could simply state that a business in a particular sector and/or with a particular number of employees can claim a specific portion of their total turnover as expenses (perhaps calculated from the median stated on previous tax returns), thus overnight stripping away the need to keep receipts and the massive accountancy industry that adds little to the delivery of goods and services in a nation.

Legitimising small-scale shadow work

Some 55 per cent of all work in the shadow economy consists of small-scale intermittent work conducted for and by kin, neighbours, friends and acquaintances, often with a social or redistributive rationale (Williams, 2004a, 2006). For example, friends or kin are often paid on a cash-in-hand basis for doing some home

Rich Aunt Agatha scheme, Netherlands

It is widely recognised that many start-ups in business secure their venture capital not from formal but from informal sources such as family, friends and acquaintances. A resulting problem is that these loans are often made on a relatively informal basis, which may contribute to an attitude from the outset that informal practices are part of the culture of the enterprise that is being established. Furthermore, contracts may not be enforceable and will often not be written down. In the Netherlands, this was recognised. As a result, a scheme called the Tante Agaath-Regeling ('Rich Aunt Agatha Arrangement') was introduced. This provides an incentive to those making loans and, in doing so, helps those using personal loans from family and friends (Aunt Agatha) to start off on the right footing. By exempting these private moneylenders from certain taxes, the intention is that, if such loans are put on to the radar screen of the tax authorities but still not taxable, it is more likely to encourage businesses to start off on a more formal basis rather than seeing themselves as being engaged in informal arrangements which might well carry over into everyday trading practices (Renooy et al., 2004; Williams, 2004d). So far as is known, no formal evaluation of this initiative appears to have been conducted.

improvement task (such as decorating) or child-minding as a way of providing them with some money in a manner that avoids any connotation of charity. Much of this could be legitimised overnight if it was decided that people could earn up to a certain amount each year tax-free and without declaration. This would also prevent governments from stifling active citizenship which it is so desperate to nurture in other policy realms.

In Slovenia, this was achieved by creating a simplified regulatory environment for small jobs whereby supplementary personal work, such as tasks in the household, were deemed free of taxation and other levies to a certain extent. Given that it is similarly the case in many other countries that people often feel they have no option but to conduct such small jobs as undeclared work, owing not least to the perceived problems involved in declaring it, legitimising such work is one way forward. For the unemployed, meanwhile, participation in such endeavour could be covered by allowing them to include such earnings in an annual (rather than weekly) benefits disregard.

This approach of using 'disregards' does not only have to apply to small-scale work. It could also be used in respect of the provision of capital by family and friends to start up businesses. One example of this is a scheme in the Netherlands, described in the box, which allows family and friends to make loans to new businesses.

Tax and social security incentives to deter entry into the shadow economy, however, do not have to be provided solely by the state. Civil society, professional associations, trade bodies or businesses might also be able to assist the formalisation of the shadow economy, as was seen in Romania and is described in the following box.

Micro-enterprise development programmes

Another way of encouraging legitimate start-ups is through micro-enterprise development programmes (MDPs). These provide

Builders' Social House, Romania

In Romania, the 'Construction Sector Social Agreement for 2007–2009' (Acordul Social Sectorial Pentru Construcţii 2007–2009) estimates that approximately one third of the active workforce is undeclared and highlights the importance of tackling this sphere. The Builders' Social House (Casa Socială a Constructorilor, CSC) is one prominent initiative being used to enable declared work. The CSC was established in 1998 as a privately run welfare organisation, to which the representative trade unions and employer organisations in the construction and building materials sector contribute in equal measure. It provides welfare during the cold season (1 November–31 March) when the construction sector slumbers to people who are in registered formal jobs and, in doing so, provides an incentive for workers to be in declared rather than undeclared work in the construction and building materials sector. CSC members are construction companies and manufacturers of building materials. Entitlement to welfare provision during these winter months is available only to declared employees – that is, those with employment contracts recorded with the local labour inspectorates, and whose social security contributions have been paid. Corporate contributors pay 1.5 per cent of their turnover into the CSC scheme and employees contribute 1 per cent of their gross base salary.

In 2008, CSC had 573 member organisations accounting for 40 per cent of all employment in the construction and building materials industries. During the 2007/08 winter period, 102,387 benefited from this scheme as welfare recipients. This idea is potentially transferable both to other economic sectors where work is largely seasonal, such as agriculture and forestry, and also to other countries.

micro-credit, advice, training and/or support to start-up ventures (Jurik, 2005). Although some MDPs are lending-oriented, others are more training- or advice-oriented. Evaluations of MDPs in the advanced economies have found them to be effective at promoting business growth, creating jobs and increasing clients' incomes, self-esteem and community involvement. At the same time, they also appear to help smooth the transition from unemployment to self-employment (Balkin, 1989). In Poland, for example, such a micro-enterprise development programme has been introduced targeted at young people.

In 2005 the Polish government initiated the 'First Business' programme as a supplement to the 'First Job' programme. 'First Job' was designed to boost youth employment but 'First Business' focused on nurturing entrepreneurship and self-employment among the younger generations. The First Business programme promotes entrepreneurship among young persons (high school graduates younger than 25 and university graduates younger than 27) and helps them create and run their own business or start working as a self-employed person. The programme provides theoretical courses on setting up and running an enterprise, gives practical training in matters related to entrepreneurship, and provides loans and subsidies from the Labour Fund (Fundusz Pracy) and from the Bank of Domestic Economy (Bank Gospodarstwa Krajowego). The main focus of the programme is to offer young entrepreneurs real assistance in setting up and conducting a business and not just to give them financial aid.

This programme in Poland is similar to many other MDPs. As yet, little is known about whether such MDPs are effective in helping fledgling micro-enterprises to start up legitimately. By providing formal loans, for example, MDPs might well help businesses to launch their operations on a formal footing. If such formal loans are also coupled with advice, support and training, the likelihood of such ventures starting off on a formal footing could be further enhanced.

Smoothing the transition to self-employment

Unemployed people often represent only a small proportion of all persons engaged in the shadow economy (e.g. Jensen et al., 1995; Leonard, 1998; Pahl, 1984; Renooy, 1990; Williams, 2004a, 2004b, 2004c). Despite this, a vast amount of energy and attention is devoted to tackling the unemployed engaged in the shadow economy. The result has been many initiatives to ease the transition from unemployment to self-employment. Less attention has been paid to easing the transition from employment to self-employment, despite the evidence that the vast majority of the newly self-employed have previously been employees rather than unemployed (Williams, 2007) and that those in formal employment often start up their business ventures on an 'on-the-side' undeclared basis in the first instance (Williams, 2008). This lack of attention to smoothing the transition from employment to legitimate self-employment is a major gap in policy that still needs to be addressed.

Encouraging movement out of the shadow economy

To 'pull' businesses and workers out of the shadow economy, measures can be targeted either at the shadow workforce itself or the hirers of such labour. These measures fall into a number of different categories.

Society-wide amnesties

Society-wide amnesties have been used to tackle the shadow economy in many countries (e.g. Hasseldine, 1998; López Laborda and Rodrigo, 2003; Torgler and Schaltegger, 2005). In Italy, for example, a six-month amnesty in 2001 generated €1.4 billion additional tax revenue, which constituted 0.4 per cent of total tax revenue (Torgler and Schaltegger, 2005). Another amnesty in Italy in 2003 resulted in 703,000 illegal immigrants coming forward, 48.6 per cent of whom were women employed in shadow work as domestic workers and care providers (Ghezzi, 2009). Indeed, since 1982, more than sixty amnesty programmes have been conducted in the USA with strong variations in the repatriated revenues across different states (Torgler and Schaltegger, 2005). In a comprehensive review of 43 of these tax amnesties pursued in 35 US states between 1982 and 1997, Hasseldine (1998) shows that the collection rate ranged from 0.008 to 2.6 per cent of total tax revenues.

One option might be to consider an amnesty which would allow undeclared activities to gradually move towards legitimisation over a transition period of, say, two years, without involving any sanctions. At the end of the period stronger sanctions would be introduced for those who continue to work in the shadow economy (European Parliament Committee on Employment and Social Affairs, 2008: 7).

Voluntary disclosure

Another policy option is to offer amnesties on an individual basis to those voluntarily disclosing that they have been working in the shadow economy. An example of voluntary disclosure is the

'VAT short-term incentive' scheme in the UK, offering people the opportunity to regularise their value added tax (VAT) situation. From April to September 2003, it ran a short-term one-off incentive scheme for businesses that should have registered for VAT but had not. The government forecast that 6,300 businesses would take advantage of the scheme and raise £11 million in additional VAT and interest. Penalties would be waived so long as the business continued to comply for twelve months. The scheme cost £500,000 in advertising costs and an estimated £2.7 million in penalties forgone from businesses which would have registered anyway. When the scheme closed, the department had received 3,000 registrations which raised £11.4 million in tax and interest or an average of £3,800 per case. Around 55 per cent of businesses taking advantage of the scheme subsequently failed to submit a VAT return, causing the department to impose £2.5 million in penalties. This had a return-to-cost ratio of 23:1 compared with 4.5:1 overall for all hidden economy compliance activity in the UK (NAO, 2008).

Another voluntary disclosure initiative, again in the UK, involved offshore bank accounts. In 2006 and 2007, the UK government won a ruling that required financial institutions to disclose the details of offshore bank accounts held by UK residents. As a result, Her Majesty's Revenue and Customs (HMRC) received details of 400,000 bank accounts from which it is estimated that up to 100,000 people should have included income and/or the resulting interest from those accounts on their tax return but had not. HMRC used a voluntary disclosure initiative to encourage people to come forward and disclose and pay all tax owed on their foreign bank accounts. By June 2007, the closing date of the scheme, HMRC had received 64,000 notifications and around 45,000 people came forward to disclose under the arrangements, bringing in a return of some £400 million at a cost of £6 million, or a return of 67:1 (ibid.). Belgium ran similar voluntary disclosure schemes on offshore banking in both 2004 and 2005, as has the Australian Tax Office.

Voluntary disclosure schemes could be introduced in other spheres such as home repair, maintenance and improvement, as well as among landlords. These might be generic campaigns or might also involve more targeted campaigns whereby information is obtained through data matching on potentially non-compliant groups and then that information is used to contact those who might wish to consider taking advantage of the voluntary disclosure option. Lessons could be learned from other countries regarding the use of appeals and notification letters (see further below).

There is a strong economic case for amnesties and/or voluntary disclosure in terms of the incentives they create. There may be individuals who wish to regularise their business activities after they have started their business in the shadow economy. To approach the tax authorities to do so, however, would involve tacitly admitting to previous evasion and could lead to harsh (and unpredictable) penalties. Of course, amnesties cannot be used with predictable regularity or there would be fewer incentives to work in the formal economy: small businesses could begin by evading tax knowing that an amnesty could be granted at some stage.

Advisory and support services

It is now commonly recognised that the kind of business advice

The CUORE initiative in Naples, Italy

CUORE (*Centri Urbani Operativi per la Riqualificazione Economica*), or Operative Urban Centre for Economic Upgrading, started in 1999 with an agreement between the municipality of Naples and the University Frederico II to research the local business environment. This research revealed that the principal local labour market problem in Naples was not unemployment but the hidden economy. Today, CUORE consists of a network of neighbourhood service centres for entrepreneurs and would-be entrepreneurs. Each local CUORE centre services a low-income neighbourhood and their target group is small and micro-sized hidden entrepreneurs with the potential for growth. Once these are identified, CUORE centres offer information and advice to aid formalisation (Bàculo, 2001, 2002, 2005).

Following a request by an undeclared worker, CUORE operators devise custom-made regularisation and development paths. The project workers closely monitor each step in the process to make sure that the enterprise follows the agreed path towards regularisation and that the path still suits the needs of the enterprise. Project workers tend to be familiar with the neighbourhood. In total, according to Bàculo (2005), some 1,280 hidden enterprises have received counselling and 326 problems have been solved.

Besides providing advice and support, attempts have also been made to provide incentives for businesses to formalise. Business consortia have been established to provide promotional aid and training, arrange trade fairs, help protect the originality of labels and to provide aid with the internationalisation of markets. This provides additional positive reasons for legitimising a business and creates an environment in which businesses can compete on grounds other than labour cost so as to reduce the necessity for hidden practices to reduce labour costs (Comitato per l'emersione del lavoro no regolare, 2003).

Since the Naples experiment, this initiative has been replicated elsewhere in Italy.

and support required by those seeking to legitimise their business ventures differs from that required by start-up or growth businesses who wish to go through a formal business planning process (Caianello and Voltura, 2003; Copisarow, 2004; Copisarow and Barbour, 2004; ILO, 2002; Meldolesi and Ruvolo, 2003; Small Business Council, 2004; Williams, 2005). It is also acknowledged that support and advice is generally not widely available to them at present about how they might resolve their situation (Copisarow and Barbour, 2004; ILO, 2002; Small Business Council, 2004; Williams, 2005). The development of a 'formalisation service' is one way forward. The CUORE initiative (see box) was also set up to provide enterprises with help and advice on formalisation.

Other initiatives, however, have been less successful. In the UK, a pilot 'formalisation service' implemented in 2005 in Hartlepool in the north-east of England was based on Her Majesty's Revenue and Customs 'offering' to individuals engaged in the shadow economy a confidential and anonymous assessment of their existing liabilities. If the individuals concerned accepted and paid the assessment of their liabilities, their activities would be 'legitimised' and they would be reintegrated into the formal economy with no legal action taken against them. Only one individual came forward and undertook a review of their liabilities. The subsequent evaluation found a lack of knowledge of the scheme, low levels of trust between the target group and the authorities, the wording of the campaign unappealing and a failure to use an independent body for people to approach, such as the local Citizens Advice Bureau (Centre for Economic and Social Inclusion, 2006).

A further example of advisory and support services for

legitimising the shadow economy is found in Australia. Many nations provide written advice, guidance and training on the records businesses need to keep for tax purposes. The Australian Tax Office, however, has gone one step farther by providing free record-keeping software, a record-keeping assessment computer tool to help small businesses understand the business records they need to keep and which evaluates how well the business is doing, and fact sheets for specific sectors on basic record-keeping requirements. The provision of this level of advice and support is replicable in many other nations.

Targeting customers with indirect tax measures

One way of encouraging consumers and businesses to use legitimate rather than shadow work is to reduce value added tax (VAT) on specific goods and services where the shadow economy is widespread; this could include areas such as the household repair, maintenance and improvement sector (see Capital Economics, 2003). Whether VAT reductions might lead to the increased formalisation of the shadow economy, however, is open to debate. Although early academic research argued that the introduction of VAT had little effect on the extent of the shadow economy (Bhattacharyya, 1990; Feige, 1990; Frey and Weck, 1983; Macafee, 1980), few contemporary evaluations have analysed whether this is actually the case.

Despite this, some EU member states have taken up the opportunity offered by Directive 1999/85/EC to reduce VAT on specific labour-intensive services. In the sphere of building renovation and maintenance, for example, several member states (such as Finland, Sweden and Italy) have opted for a reduction in VAT.

Nevertheless, and as the European Commission (2007: 7) asserts, 'There is limited evidence of the employment creating effect of a single reduction of VAT.'

Targeting consumers with direct tax measures and wage cost subsidies

Although general reductions in the rates of income tax might be used to try to cure the prevalence of the shadow economy, this topic, as has been noted, will not be discussed in this chapter because it has much wider implications. More targeted strategies, however, are available. One option is to give straightforward income tax relief, claimed on (self-assessed) tax returns, to customers using declared labour to do specific household tasks (for example, childcare and cleaning). Tax rebates on home maintenance expenses have been available in France since 2000, along with tax reductions for house repairs in Italy and Luxembourg.

An increasingly popular initiative which is being used to tackle the shadow economy is the use of vouchers which can be combined with the tax relief approach. One such initiative which has proved successful is the *Chèque Emploi Service Universel* (CESU) scheme, which was introduced in France to simplify the process of hiring and paying a domestic worker. The worker's salary is paid using a system of cheques, which can be purchased at the local bank. The benefit for the customer is that they can claim an income tax reduction that amounts to 50 per cent of the sum spent on purchasing the cheques. For the supplier, meanwhile, the salary cannot be less than the national minimum wage, and a 10 per cent indemnity is also given for paid leave. By 2002, the number of households legally using domestic service workers was some 765,411 while the number of full-time equivalent jobs created was just under 88,000 (Adjerad, 2003). By 2002, 53 per cent of all formal employers of domestic workers used the scheme (ibid.). An estimated 20 per cent of those previously working on an undeclared basis are now officially employed (Le Feuvre, 2000).

Of course, we need to be careful how far we extend such schemes. Some activities such as childcare often attract tax relief in any case and tying such tax relief to the use of non-shadow labour is not an especially significant step. In general, high tax rates distort the economy and reduce the division of labour and use of paid labour with respect to household tasks such as childcare, gardening and cleaning. Although economists generally oppose specific tax relief measures, there can be a case for the creation of limited tax relief measures in certain fields of activity, and it may be possible to tie such measures to assisting the formalisation of the shadow economy.

Commitment to tax morality

A wealth of research reveals that low tax morality leads to larger shadow economies (Alm et al., 1995; Alm and Torgler, 2006; Riahi-Belkaoui, 2004; Richardson, 2006). Measures to improve commitment to paying taxes, therefore, are important when tackling shadow work. Indeed, beliefs and attitudes towards the shadow economy more strongly correlate with compliance than do deterrence factors (Carroll, 1987; Etzioni, 1988; Murphy, 2005, 2008; Roth et al., 1989; Smith, 1990). Riahi-Belkaoui (2004), examining 30 countries, identifies that tax compliance is strongly correlated with high moral norms, as does Richardson (2006) in his comparison of 45 countries. Alm et al. (1995) and Alm and Torgler (2006) similarly compare the extent of the shadow economy and the level of tax morale across various countries and find strong evidence that societal attitudes towards tax compliance exert a measurable and significant impact on individual behaviour.

In this commitment approach, therefore, the desire is to engender commitment to tax morality so that 'sticks' and 'carrots' are not needed. Put another way, there is a shift from direct to indirect controls, or from compliance to commitment. To achieve this, a variety of measures can be employed.

One tactic for engendering commitment to tax morality so as to reduce the shadow economy is to run awareness-raising and information campaigns. Such campaigns can either:

- Inform undeclared workers of the costs and risks.
- Inform potential users of undeclared labour of the risks and costs.
- Inform undeclared workers of the benefits of formalisation, such as increasing their credibility as business people and opening up business opportunities for them; and/or
- Inform potential users of the shadow economy of the benefits of formal labour.

Until now, it has perhaps been the case that most publicity campaigns have focused upon the costs and risks of participating in the shadow economy. As Thurman et al. (1984) highlight, however, this is ineffective because individuals neutralise their guilt about engaging in the shadow economy, for example by regarding the adverse consequences of tax evasion as being the result of others' behaviour. As such, awareness-raising and information campaigns should perhaps focus upon the benefits of formal work, not the risks and costs of the shadow economy.

In the UK, an evaluation of the advertising campaigns run by HMRC reveals that some 8,300 additional people had registered to pay tax who would otherwise not have done so. They will pay tax of around £38 million over three years, providing a return of 19:1 on the expenditure of £2 million (NAO, 2008). This compares with an overall return of 4.5:1 on the £41 million a year spent on all HMRC's hidden economy work in 2006/07 (ibid.). It therefore appears that advertising campaigns are relatively effective in terms of value for money.

The question of whether normative appeals are more effective at eliciting compliant behaviour is open to debate. Although Blumenthal et al. (2001), examining experience in the US state of Minnesota, reveal that normative appeals affected only some groups of taxpayers, and Chung and Trivedi (2003) find that friendly persuasion is effective, it depends on the nature of the appeal made. Hasseldine et al. (2007) examine 7,300 sole proprietors in the UK. Comparing the effect of five different letters ranging from a simple offer of assistance to a letter advising that his/her tax return had been preselected for audit, they find that tax compliance appeals resulted in greater compliance, particularly among those who do not use a paid preparer. Sanction appeals, however, were found to be more effective than normative appeals.

Their effectiveness, therefore, depends not only on the nature of the appeal. It is also influenced by the individuals to whom the appeal is addressed, including their perceptions of the social norms, the fairness of the tax system and whether there is perceived procedural justice in tax administration. In relation to the individuals addressed and their perceptions of social norms, Wenzel (2005a) finds that tax ethics causally affect tax compliance and also that tax ethics are themselves affected by compliance levels. He also finds that perceived social norms causally affect personally held tax ethics, but only for respondents who identified strongly with their respective group. Furthermore, perceived social norms causally affect tax compliance. Wenzel (2005b) also reveals that misperceptions of social norms can have a significant impact on tax compliance. If the shadow economy is viewed as extensive, tax compliance declines. Wenzel (2004b) finds in Australia that, when taxpayers strongly identify with the group to whom social norms (ethics and morality attributed to other taxpayers) are attached, they internalise the social norms and act accordingly. If tax morality is perceived as high, they thus engage in tax-compliant behaviour. In contrast, if morality is seen as low, non-compliance increases.

The perceived fairness and justice of the tax system and administration also have a significant impact on tax morality and compliance (Wenzel, 2002). 'Fairness' refers to the extent to which individuals believe that they are paying their fair share compared with others (Kinsey and Gramsick, 1993; Wenzel, 2004b); 'justice' refers to whether citizens receive the goods and services they believe that they deserve given the taxes that they pay (Kinsey and Gramsick, 1993; Kinsey et al., 1991; Mason and Calvin, 1984; Richardson and Sawyer, 2001; Scholz and Lubell, 1998; Thurman et al., 1984); and 'procedural justice' refers to the degree to which people believe that the tax authority has treated them in a respectful, impartial and responsible manner (Braithwaite and Reinhart, 2000; Murphy, 2005; Tyler, 1997; Wenzel, 2002). As Murphy (2005) finds, people who feel they have been treated in a procedurally fair manner by an organisation will be more likely to trust that organisation and more inclined to accept its decisions and follow its directions.

It is worth noting again that there is a danger, once the shadow economy starts growing, that tax morale falls. This might lead to further growth in the shadow economy and then increases in tax rates as governments try to maintain revenues. The increases in tax rates might be associated with more evasion and might also be accompanied by more tax complexity as governments try to exempt specific groups or activities from the increased burden of tax. Both increased complexity and perceived arbitrariness and higher levels of evasion may, in turn, reduce tax morale further.

Shifting towards an approach whereby the tax authorities promote commitment by the citizen requires a fundamental shift in the organisational cultures of tax administrations. Braithwaite (2002) distinguishes between 'regulatory formalism' and 'responsive regulation'. The former is where an agency lists its problems in advance, specifies the appropriate response and generates manuals of rules to achieve these responses. This arguably enables process efficiency and outcome consistency to be achieved. In recent years, the nature of regulatory formalism has been revised by shifting away from relying mainly on deterrence and towards the use of incentives to engage in legitimate work. There has also been a greater consideration of the fair and respectful treatment of taxpayers (Braithwaite, 2007). Such 'humanising' of regulatory formalism, however, is not the same as responsive regulation or what is also here termed a commitment approach.

'Responsive regulation is a process that ... openly engages taxpayers to think about their obligations and accept responsibility for regulating themselves in a manner that is consistent with the law' (ibid.: 6). It is about winning their 'hearts and minds' so as to engender a culture of commitment to tax morality in order that people will regulate themselves and not need to be regulated by external rules. Until now, it is governments outside Europe which have been pioneering this approach, prominently Australia and New Zealand. In an evaluation of the difficulties involved in developing such a commitment approach, Job et al. (2007) find that, in introducing this culture change in Australia, New Zealand and East Timor, the major challenges faced by the tax administrations were: resistance to change; meeting the legal principles of consistency and equity; allowing staff discretion while avoiding corruption; recognition of different occupational skill sets; and the lack of an appropriate language to present the new ideas. To shift from compliance to commitment, or what might be termed direct to indirect controls, requires a fundamental shift in organisational culture within the government departments responsible for tackling the shadow economy. It also requires a generally accepted tax system that is straightforward and widely regarded as fair.

Combining various policy approaches and measures

The policy approaches and measures considered above are not mutually exclusive. For example, governments might simplify regulatory compliance as well as introduce incentives, such as amnesties, to enable people to enter the legitimate realm. At the same time, in relation to those who fail to comply, they may implement tougher sanctions for those subsequently caught while also introducing campaigns to elicit greater commitment among the public to tax morality. At present, for example, measures to improve detection through inspections are often combined with campaigns aimed at raising awareness or warnings that inspections are about to occur. Amnesty and voluntary disclosure schemes, meanwhile, are frequently followed by tougher sanctions. Whether these combinations are more effective than other combinations, however, has not so far been evaluated.

There are also various ways of sequencing policy measures, some of which might be more effective than others. The Australian government, in its 'responsive regulation' approach, for example, uses commitment measures in the first instance to facilitate compliance, followed by persuasion and only then punitive measures to tackle tax non-compliance (Braithwaite, 2007; Job et al., 2007). Thus the tax authority starts with the least intrusive measures and then moves on to more intrusive approaches.

The idea is that a tax authority that is legitimate and engaging seriously with the democratic will of the people should not need, in most cases, to pursue the coercion option to win compliance. This approach also recognises that compliance is influenced by many factors – business, industry, sociological, economic and psychological – all of which shape whether a person engages in the shadow economy. The outcome is recognition of a continuum of attitudes towards compliance and different policy responses that can be temporally sequenced starting with commitment measures and moving through to sanctions.

10 CONCLUSION

As we have seen, measuring the shadow economy is extremely difficult. Nevertheless, it is possible using modern statistical techniques to estimate its size with a reasonable degree of confidence.

The size of the shadow economy might have surprised some readers if they had seen these estimates two or three years ago. The evidence suggests, for example, that the shadow economy constitutes around 20 per cent of national income in Italy, Spain and Greece. The recent euro crisis, however, has shone a spotlight on problems in these countries with regard to tax collection and compliance and the problems are now more widely known.

The causes of the shadow economy include tax and social security burdens, tax morale, the quality of state institutions, labour market regulation, the level of transfer payments and the quality of public services. The first two in this list are empirically substantially more important than the others.

The level of shadow economic activity does not necessarily cause direct reductions in economic welfare. Economic activity is, after all, economic activity. Whether it is declared or not it still raises people's incomes. The money earned in the shadow economy is often immediately spent in the formal economy. It is therefore important not to try to stamp out the shadow economy by stamping out the economic activity that goes with it – throwing the baby out with the bathwater, so to speak. This is an important consideration when we look at potential solutions.

While the size of the shadow economy might surprise some people, perhaps even more surprising is the number of people involved and how widespread is the acceptance of shadow work. As an example of its scope, it is notable that about thirty million people undertake shadow work in the EU; around half of all construction workers in Germany undertake shadow work; and over 80 per cent of all Danes find shadow work acceptable – at least in some circumstances.

When it comes to thinking about policies to reduce the shadow economy, the disaggregated evidence on those involved has to be considered carefully. In fact, there is little evidence that illegal immigration is a significant contributory factor to the shadow economy in general, though illegal migrants constitute a relatively high proportion of total employees in Greece and the USA. One important split is that between the unemployed and the employed. If shadow work is mainly undertaken by the unemployed, policies should mainly focus on the welfare system. Welfare-to-work schemes might help reduce the incentive to undertake shadow work while receiving benefits, for example, as would income disregards. On the other hand, if shadow work is mainly undertaken by the employed, it is important to ensure that the tax and business registration systems encourage compliance rather than make compliance difficult. The situation differs in different parts of Europe. In Nordic countries, shadow work is much more common among the employed than among the unemployed. In western Europe, shadow work tends to be more or less equally common among the employed and the unemployed in terms of numbers of people involved, though the employed undertake a greater amount of shadow work. There are no disaggregated data for the UK.

There is an extremely high level of shadow work in less developed countries. The nature of what is better described as 'informal' work in this context, however, is very different from that in OECD countries. In general, the problems lie with the legal systems that make it difficult for businesses and individuals to register their activity. Indeed, in some sectors, informality in business and employment relationships can effectively become the norm. The main focus of our detailed discussion and policy recommendations relates to the OECD. Though we have presented an analysis of the extent of the informal economy in less developed countries, we do not take this further.

When it comes to addressing the shadow economy, we can think in terms of 'meta' solutions or in terms of detailed policy recommendations. As mentioned earlier, an increased tax burden can lead to an increase in the size of the shadow economy and reduced state revenues. This, in turn, reduces the quality and quantity of publicly provided goods and services and an increase in tax rates for firms and individuals. These factors may lead to lower tax morale and a need for still higher tax rates. Reversing this vicious circle could be an important policy and, when thinking about the size of public spending and taxation as a proportion of national income, the relationship with the shadow economy should not be ignored. There are, however, much wider considerations, of course, when setting the overall level of taxation, and we do not consider the aggregate tax burden in any further detail as a potential policy measure to deal with the shadow economy.

Marginal tax rates, other non-wage costs and benefit withdrawal rules may be more relevant policy instruments than the aggregate tax burden, especially when addressing shadow work among those in employment. There is a high level of such costs in the EU – averaging 39 per cent for individuals in the bottom half of the income spectrum. In the UK the 'low wage trap' is especially large: individuals moving from low to median wages lose a high proportion of any wage increment in taxes or lost benefits. This is another problem that should be examined when considering how to reduce the size of the shadow economy.

Research also shows that shadow economies are smaller in countries with fewer laws and regulations combined with consistent enforcement, and where there is less bribery and corruption in the economic system. This provides a further argument for ensuring good-quality legal institutions. At a more detailed level, however, governments should put more emphasis on legalising certain shadow economy activities or on making formalisation much easier. Such 'pull' measures – so called because they pull shadow work into the formal economy rather than try to eliminate it – are of three types: preventive measures that seek to prevent entry into the shadow economy; curative measures that seek to move those currently engaged in shadow work out of this sphere and into the legitimate realm; and measures that seek to improve commitment to tax morality.

Many examples of such measures are discussed in the earlier chapters. We will reiterate three of those examples here. It is possible that much could be achieved by copying the example of the 'On the Spot' firm as used in Portugal, which makes company registration very straightforward. Business start-up loans given by relatives and friends could also be brought into the formal economy by copying the 'Rich Aunt Agatha' scheme used in the Netherlands. This scheme allows small loans to be provided without taxes and ensures that a small business can set off on the right footing. This is very important because, once a business has evaded taxes, formalising the business can be quite difficult through fear of penalties for past evasion. Amnesties could also be a very promising policy initiative in dealing with this specific problem. Amnesties cannot be used frequently and predictably, but they should be in the policy toolkit. Such amnesties tend to have a high return-to-cost ratio.

The shadow economy is more pervasive than is perhaps widely thought, its measurement is difficult and successful policy solutions are not always easy to implement. This monograph, however, has suggested how to turn the tide. It is necessary to have high tax morale combined with a tax system that is coherent and works with – rather than against – the grain of human nature. This relates not just to the size of the tax burden but to the particular incentives that apply to specific groups within society when they undertake more work or earn more money. In addition, a range of more detailed policy approaches can be taken. In many senses these 'micro-measures' are 'win-win' policies in that they cost relatively little money and just involve ensuring that there is a sensible regulatory and legal framework within which business should operate. If this monograph starts to encourage governments to adopt such approaches, then it will have achieved its objective.

Appendix 1
ADJUSTMENTS TO NATIONAL ACCOUNTS TO INCORPORATE THE SHADOW ECONOMY

Owing to the big increase in the size of the shadow economy in value-added terms, a number of countries adjust their national accounts to include estimates of shadow economic activity.[1] The OECD (2011: 14) has detected seven activities that could lead to appropriate adjustments being made by some countries in their national accounts (see box).

Some countries make very large adjustments to their national accounts. For example, the adjustment made by Italy is between 14.8 and 16.7 per cent of national income and in Poland between 7.8 and 15.7 per cent. The largest adjustment is in the national accounts of Russia with 24.3 per cent and the smallest in the USA with 0.8 per cent. Table 25 clearly shows that countries make adjustments in very different ways, which will make it more difficult to compare national income figures.

Table 26 shows national income per capita data for a selection of countries. The second column shows published national income data. The third column adjusts for the shadow economy estimates in Table 6 assuming that the quoted figure did not include an adjustment for the shadow economy. The fourth column provides an estimate of the true size of the economy, under the assumption that the declared adjustment to official national income figures for

---

1   This section, including the box and tables, closely follows OECD (2011: 11–12, Box 2).

Activities in respect of which adjustments to national accounts could be made

A1: A producer deliberately does not register in order to avoid tax and social security obligations.

A2: A producer deliberately does not register as a legal identity or as an entrepreneur because he is involved in illegal activities.

A3: A producer is not required to register because he has no market output.

A4: A legal person is not surveyed for reasons such as the business register being out of date or because updating procedures are inadequate.

A5: Registered entrepreneurs may not be surveyed because of the failure of the statistical office to conduct a survey of registered entrepreneurs.

A6: Cross-output is under-reported and/or intermediate consumption is overstated.

A7: Data are either not complete or not collected or not directly collectable and/or data are incorrectly handled.

the size of the shadow economy had been made. It can be seen that, though the rankings do not change greatly, the estimate of the size of the underlying economy depends substantially on the assumptions that are made about the size of the shadow economy and the size of any adjustment that has been made to official figures. The published figure for Italy's official national income is rebased to 100 and all other figures are relative to that.

In general, the inclusion of the shadow economy brings the national income figures for different countries closer together because, except insofar as the Scandinavian countries are

Table 25 **Adjustment of non-observed economy in national accounts**

		Activities for which adjustments are made		
	Size of non-observed economy (% of GDP)	A1 Non-registered producers	A2 Non-registered identity of a producer	A3 No requirement to register
Australia	1.3			X
Austria	7.9	X		X
Belgium	3.0–4.0	X		X
Canada	Not stated	X	X	X
Czech Republic	4.6(E); 6.6(I); 9.3(O)	X	X	X
Estonia	9.6	X	X	
Finland	Not stated	X		X
Germany	Not stated			
Hungary	11.9	X	X	X
Ireland	4.0			X
Italy	14.8(L); 16.7(U)	X		X
Mexico	12.1		X	X
Netherlands	1.0			
Norway	2.4(O);1.0(E)			X
Poland	15.7(O); 7.8(E)	X	X	X
Russia	24.3	X		X
Spain	11.2	X		
Sweden	1.0		X	
Turkey	1.66	X		X
UK	Not stated	X		X
US	0.8			

Notes: The adjustments quoted are not necessarily for the same year, but they all relate to around the year 2000. O = according to output approach; E = according to expenditure approach; I = according to income approach; L = lower limit estimate; U = upper limit estimate. X means that an adjustment is made for this type of activity with the definitions relating to the definitions in the box on page 145.
Source: UN (2008), quoted in OECD (2011: 12, Table 2)

Activities for which adjustments are made			
A4 Non-registration due to old state	A5 Not captured by the stat. office	A6 Under-reporting of output	A7 Incorrect data
		✗	✗
✗	✗	✗	✗
		✗	✗
		✗	✗
✗	✗	✗	✗
		✗	✗
		✗	
		✗	✗
✗		✗	✗
✗	✗	✗	
		✗	✗
✗	✗	✗	✗
		✗	✗
✗	✗	✗	✗
✗		✗	✗
		✗	✗
		✗	
	✗	✗	✗
		✗	

concerned, a higher shadow economy tends to be associated with a lower level of national income. There are, however, significant potential anomalies, lack of consistency and lack of clarity in published data. If national income figures are not adjusted for the size of the shadow economy, misleading comparisons between countries will be made. At the same time, when comparing countries, if it is not known whether countries have made adjustments to their official data and allowances are not made for the different adjustments that different countries make, comparisons between the national income performance of different countries will also be flawed. This is even more true, of course, for less developed countries that can have very large shadow or informal economies, the size of which is very difficult to estimate.

Table 26 **National income figures and adjustments for the size of the shadow economy**

Country	Official national income per head in PPP terms*	Official national income per head plus estimate of shadow economy	National income per head including shadow economy assuming adjustment had been made to published figures
USA	151.1	163.8	163.8
Sweden	130.9	150.1	148.7
Austria	129.7	140.1	129.8
UK	114.3	126.9	126.9
Japan	109.8	121.1	121.1
Ireland	103.0	116.2	111.7
Italy	100	121.2	105.6

*http://databank.worldbank.org/databank/download/GNIPC.pdf

Appendix 2
THE SIZE OF THE SHADOW ECONOMY WORLDWIDE

Table 27 **Size and development of the shadow economy of 162 countries (% of national income)**

No.	Country	1999	2000	2001	2002	2003	2004	2005	2006	2007	Country average
1	Albania	35.7	35.3	34.9	34.7	34.4	33.9	33.7	33.3	32.9	34.3
2	Algeria	34.2	34.1	33.8	33.3	32.5	31.7	31.1	31.0	31.2	32.5
3	Angola	48.8	48.8	48.4	47.4	47.3	47.1	45.0	44.0	42.1	46.5
4	Argentina	25.2	25.4	26.1	27.6	26.4	25.5	24.7	23.8	23.0	25.3
5	Armenia	46.6	46.3	45.4	44.5	43.9	43.6	42.7	42.1	41.1	44.0
6	Australia	14.4	14.3	14.3	14.1	13.9	13.7	13.7	13.7	13.5	14.0
7	Austria	10.0	9.8	9.7	9.8	9.8	9.8	9.8	9.6	9.5	9.8
8	Azerbaijan	61.0	60.6	60.3	60.0	59.1	58.6	56.7	54.0	52.0	58.0
9	Bahamas, The	26.3	26.2	26.4	26.5	27.0	27.4	26.7	26.2	26.2	26.5
10	Bahrain	18.6	18.4	18.2	18.0	17.8	17.4	17.1	–	–	17.9
11	Bangladesh	36.0	35.6	35.5	35.7	35.6	35.5	35.1	34.5	34.1	35.3
12	Belarus	48.3	48.1	47.9	47.6	47.0	46.1	45.2	44.2	43.3	46.4
13	Belgium	22.7	22.2	22.1	22.0	22.0	21.8	21.8	21.4	21.3	21.9
14	Belize	45.2	43.8	43.3	43.4	42.3	42.0	42.1	41.7	42.0	42.9
15	Benin	51.2	50.2	49.8	49.6	49.3	49.5	49.8	49.6	49.1	49.8
16	Bhutan	29.6	29.4	29.2	29.1	28.7	28.7	28.3	28.2	27.7	28.8
17	Bolivia	67.0	67.1	67.6	67.7	67.7	66.9	64.3	62.8	63.5	66.1
18	Bosnia & Herzegovina	34.3	34.1	34.0	33.9	33.5	33.6	33.2	32.9	32.8	33.6
19	Botswana	33.9	33.4	33.2	33.3	33.0	32.8	32.7	32.3	31.9	32.9
20	Brazil	40.8	39.8	39.9	39.9	39.6	38.6	38.4	37.8	36.6	39.0

No.	Country	Years									Country average
		1999	2000	2001	2002	2003	2004	2005	2006	2007	
21	Brunei Darussalam	31.3	31.1	31.0	30.2	29.9	31.2	31.8	30.8	31.2	30.9
22	Bulgaria	37.3	36.9	36.6	36.1	35.6	34.9	34.1	33.5	32.7	35.3
23	Burkina Faso	41.3	41.4	41.3	41.4	40.3	40.1	39.7	39.7	39.6	40.5
24	Burundi	39.1	39.5	39.6	39.4	39.6	39.6	39.7	39.6	39.6	39.5
25	Cambodia	50.4	50.1	49.6	50.0	49.2	48.8	47.8	46.8	46.0	48.7
26	Cameroon	33.3	32.8	32.4	32.1	31.7	31.6	31.6	31.4	31.4	32.0
27	Canada	16.3	16.0	15.9	15.8	15.7	15.6	15.5	15.3	15.3	15.7
28	Cape Verde	36.5	36.1	35.9	35.9	35.7	35.8	35.4	34.1	33.4	35.4
29	Central African Republic	42.8	42.6	43.1	44.0	46.9	47.3	46.9	45.9	45.1	45.0
30	Chad	45.8	46.2	45.5	45.1	44.2	41.5	41.1	41.7	42.2	43.7
31	Chile	19.9	19.8	19.6	19.6	19.4	19.1	18.9	18.7	18.5	19.3
32	China	13.2	13.1	13.0	12.9	12.8	12.6	12.5	12.2	11.9	12.7
33	Colombia	39.4	39.1	38.9	38.9	37.9	37.1	36.1	35.1	33.5	37.3
34	Comoros	39.3	39.6	39.0	37.7	37.6	39.0	38.0	38.4	39.4	38.7
35	Congo, Dem. Rep.	47.2	48.0	48.2	48.1	47.1	46.9	46.8	46.8	46.7	47.3
36	Congo, Rep.	49.5	48.2	47.2	46.8	46.8	46.2	44.7	43.3	44.6	46.4
37	Costa Rica	26.1	26.2	26.4	26.4	26.1	25.9	25.6	25.0	24.0	25.7
38	Côte d'Ivoire	41.4	43.2	44.3	45.5	46.0	46.1	46.3	46.8	47.0	45.2
39	Croatia	33.8	33.4	33.2	32.6	32.1	31.7	31.3	30.8	30.4	32.1
40	Cyprus	29.2	28.7	28.2	27.8	28.2	28.1	27.7	27.3	26.5	28.0
41	Czech Republic	19.3	19.1	18.9	18.8	18.7	18.4	17.8	17.3	17.0	18.4
42	Denmark	18.4	18.0	18.0	18.0	18.0	17.8	17.6	17.0	16.9	17.7
43	Dominican Republic	32.4	32.1	32.4	32.1	32.1	32.4	31.7	31.0	30.5	31.9
44	Ecuador	34.2	34.4	33.7	33.3	32.8	31.6	30.8	30.4	30.4	32.4
45	Egypt, Arab Rep.	35.5	35.1	35.2	35.7	35.4	35.0	34.8	34.1	33.1	34.9
46	El Salvador	46.5	46.3	46.2	45.6	45.2	44.9	44.5	43.8	43.0	45.1
47	Equatorial Guinea	32.7	32.8	32.0	31.5	31.2	30.8	30.5	30.6	30.1	31.4
48	Eritrea	38.1	40.3	39.4	39.4	40.3	40.6	40.5	41.2	41.4	40.1
49	Estonia	–	32.7	32.4	32.0	31.4	31.1	30.5	29.8	29.5	31.2
50	Ethiopia	40.6	40.3	39.5	39.6	40.1	38.6	37.7	36.3	35.1	38.6

No.	Country	Years									Country average
		1999	2000	2001	2002	2003	2004	2005	2006	2007	
51	Fiji	32.9	33.6	33.3	32.6	32.5	31.9	31.4	31.0	32.6	32.4
52	Finland	18.4	18.1	17.9	17.8	17.7	17.6	17.4	17.1	17.0	17.7
53	France	15.7	15.2	15.0	15.1	15.0	14.9	14.8	14.8	14.7	15.0
54	Gabon	46.2	48.0	47.4	47.6	47.5	48.0	47.7	48.0	47.3	47.5
55	Gambia, The	46.1	45.1	44.7	47.1	45.4	43.8	43.6	42.4	40.9	44.3
56	Georgia	68.3	67.3	67.2	67.2	65.9	65.5	65.1	63.6	62.1	65.8
57	Germany	16.4	16.0	15.9	16.1	16.3	16.1	16.0	15.6	15.3	16.0
58	Ghana	42.0	41.9	41.8	41.6	41.3	40.9	39.5	38.6	38.3	40.7
59	Greece	28.5	28.7	28.2	28.0	27.4	27.1	26.9	26.4	26.5	27.5
60	Guatemala	51.6	51.5	51.6	51.2	50.7	50.5	50.2	49.0	47.9	50.5
61	Guinea	39.7	39.6	39.3	38.7	38.8	38.5	38.4	38.9	39.2	39.0
62	Guinea-Bissau	40.4	39.6	39.6	40.7	41.5	41.9	41.7	41.5	41.6	40.9
63	Guyana	33.4	33.6	33.3	33.7	33.9	33.4	34.3	33.8	34.0	33.7
64	Haiti	54.8	55.4	56.1	56.5	56.4	57.4	57.1	57.0	57.1	56.4
65	Honduras	50.3	49.6	49.7	49.6	48.9	48.3	47.3	46.1	45.1	48.3
66	Hong Kong, China	17.0	16.6	16.6	16.6	16.4	15.9	15.5	15.0	14.7	16.0
67	Hungary	25.4	25.1	24.8	24.5	24.4	24.1	24.0	23.7	23.7	24.4
68	Iceland	16.0	15.9	15.8	16.0	15.9	15.5	15.1	15.0	15.0	15.6
69	India	23.2	23.1	22.8	22.6	22.3	22.0	21.7	21.2	20.7	22.2
70	Indonesia	19.7	19.4	19.4	19.3	19.1	18.8	18.6	18.3	17.9	18.9
71	Iran, Islamic Rep.	19.1	18.9	19.0	18.7	18.2	17.9	18.1	17.7	17.3	18.3
72	Ireland	16.1	15.9	15.9	15.9	16.0	15.8	15.6	15.5	15.4	15.8
73	Israel	22.7	21.9	22.3	22.7	22.7	22.1	21.8	21.2	20.7	22.0
74	Italy	27.8	27.1	26.7	26.8	27.0	27.0	27.1	26.9	26.8	27.0
75	Jamaica	36.4	36.4	36.2	36.2	34.4	33.9	34.0	32.9	32.5	34.8
76	Japan	11.4	11.2	11.2	11.3	11.2	10.9	10.7	10.4	10.3	11.0
77	Jordan	19.4	19.4	19.2	18.9	18.7	18.3	18.0	17.5	17.2	18.5
78	Kazakhstan	43.8	43.2	42.5	42.0	41.1	40.6	39.8	38.9	38.4	41.1
79	Kenya	33.7	34.3	34.0	34.8	34.6	33.7	32.7	31.1	29.5	33.2
80	Korea, Rep.	28.3	27.5	27.3	26.9	26.8	26.5	26.3	25.9	25.6	26.8
81	Kuwait	20.1	20.1	20.2	20.3	19.3	18.8	18.1	17.9	–	19.4
82	Kyrgyz Republic	41.4	41.2	40.8	41.4	40.5	39.8	40.1	39.8	38.8	40.4

No.	Country	1999	2000	2001	2002	2003	2004	2005	2006	2007	Country average
83	Lao PDR	30.9	30.6	30.2	30.0	29.8	29.4	28.9	28.4	28.0	29.6
84	Latvia	30.8	30.5	30.1	29.8	29.4	29.0	28.4	27.7	27.2	29.2
85	Lebanon	34.1	34.1	33.7	33.5	33.2	32.4	32.4	32.8	32.0	33.1
86	Lesotho	31.7	31.3	31.1	31.0	30.7	30.1	30.2	29.3	28.8	30.5
87	Liberia	44.2	43.2	43.2	43.1	45.0	45.4	44.9	44.5	44.2	44.2
88	Libya	34.7	35.1	34.5	33.8	34.9	33.9	33.1	32.0	30.9	33.7
89	Lithuania	33.8	33.7	33.3	32.8	32.0	31.7	31.0	30.4	29.7	32.0
90	Luxembourg	10.0	9.8	9.8	9.8	9.8	9.8	9.7	9.6	9.4	9.7
91	Macao, China	13.3	13.1	13.0	12.9	12.5	12.1	11.9	11.7	11.1	12.4
92	Macedonia	39.0	38.2	39.1	38.9	38.4	37.4	36.9	36.0	34.9	37.6
93	Madagascar	40.1	39.6	38.7	44.8	43.4	41.6	40.8	39.8	38.5	40.8
94	Malawi	39.9	40.3	42.5	44.4	43.4	42.5	42.6	41.3	39.4	41.8
95	Malaysia	32.2	31.1	31.6	31.5	31.2	30.7	30.4	30.0	29.6	30.9
96	Maldives	30.3	30.3	30.0	29.4	29.2	28.9	29.6	29.3	28.6	29.5
97	Mali	42.5	42.3	40.8	40.2	39.9	40.6	40.1	39.9	39.9	40.7
98	Malta	27.4	27.1	27.3	27.3	27.5	27.6	27.3	27.0	26.5	27.2
99	Mauritania	35.5	36.1	36.0	35.8	35.8	35.1	34.4	31.7	–	35.1
100	Mauritius	23.3	23.1	22.9	23.0	22.7	22.4	22.4	22.2	21.9	22.7
101	Mexico	30.8	30.1	30.3	30.4	30.5	30.1	29.9	29.2	28.8	30.0
102	Moldova	45.6	45.1	44.1	44.5	44.6	44.0	43.4	44.3	–	44.5
103	Mongolia	18.4	18.4	18.3	18.0	17.7	17.4	17.1	16.7	16.4	17.6
104	Morocco	36.5	36.4	35.7	35.5	35.0	34.2	34.9	33.1	33.1	34.9
105	Mozambique	41.1	40.3	40.4	39.8	39.8	39.7	38.9	38.6	–	39.8
106	Myanmar	51.6	52.6	51.5	50.7	49.0	49.1	47.8	–	–	50.3
107	Namibia	31.4	31.4	31.2	31.3	30.7	29.7	29.6	28.8	28.5	30.3
108	Nepal	37.2	36.8	36.7	37.1	36.9	36.8	36.7	36.3	36.0	36.7
109	Netherlands	13.3	13.1	13.1	13.2	13.3	13.2	13.2	13.2	13.0	13.2
110	New Zealand	13.0	12.8	12.6	12.4	12.2	12.0	12.1	12.1	12.0	12.4
111	Nicaragua	45.7	45.2	45.3	45.5	45.0	44.2	43.8	43.5	43.1	44.6
112	Niger	41.7	41.9	40.9	40.3	39.7	40.7	39.7	38.6	–	40.4
113	Nigeria	58.0	57.9	57.8	57.6	56.3	55.1	53.8	53.0	–	56.2
114	Norway	19.2	19.1	19.0	19.0	19.0	18.5	18.5	18.2	18.0	18.7
115	Oman	19.1	18.9	18.5	18.5	18.4	18.3	18.0	17.6	–	18.4
116	Pakistan	37.0	36.8	37.0	36.8	36.2	35.3	34.9	33.8	33.6	35.7
117	Panama	64.8	64.1	64.7	65.1	64.4	63.5	61.7	60.0	–	63.5

No.	Country	1999	2000	2001	2002	2003	2004	2005	2006	2007	Country average
118	Papua New Guinea	35.5	36.1	36.8	37.1	37.1	37.0	37.2	37.1	36.5	36.7
119	Paraguay	38.0	39.8	39.7	40.1	39.1	38.3	38.2	37.4	–	38.8
120	Peru	60.1	59.9	60.2	59.1	58.6	57.9	57.2	55.7	53.7	58.0
121	Philippines	43.8	43.3	43.0	42.5	42.0	41.6	40.1	39.5	38.3	41.6
122	Poland	27.7	27.6	27.7	27.7	27.5	27.3	26.9	26.4	26.0	27.2
123	Portugal	23.0	22.7	22.6	22.7	23.0	23.1	23.3	23.2	23.0	23.0
124	Qatar	–	19.0	19.3	19.0	19.6	17.4	18.4	–	–	18.8
125	Romania	34.3	34.4	33.7	33.5	32.8	32.0	31.7	30.7	30.2	32.6
126	Russian Federation	47.0	46.1	45.3	44.5	43.6	43.0	42.4	41.7	40.6	43.8
127	Rwanda	40.5	40.3	40.6	39.9	40.7	40.2	39.3	39.1	–	40.1
128	Saudi Arabia	18.7	18.4	18.7	19.2	18.3	17.7	17.4	17.4	16.8	18.1
129	Senegal	45.0	45.1	44.5	45.1	44.4	43.2	42.3	42.4	41.7	43.7
130	Sierra Leone	48.6	48.6	47.6	45.4	44.8	44.4	44.3	43.6	42.9	45.6
131	Singapore	13.3	13.1	13.3	13.3	13.1	12.8	12.7	12.4	12.2	12.9
132	Slovak Republic	18.9	18.9	18.8	18.6	18.3	18.1	17.6	17.2	16.8	18.1
133	Slovenia	27.3	27.1	26.7	26.6	26.4	26.2	25.8	25.3	24.7	26.2
134	Solomon Islands	31.7	33.4	34.5	34.8	34.7	33.8	33.4	33.2	32.7	33.6
135	South Africa	28.4	28.4	28.4	28.0	27.8	27.1	26.5	26.0	25.2	27.3
136	Spain	23.0	22.7	22.4	22.4	22.4	22.5	22.4	22.4	22.2	22.5
137	Sri Lanka	45.2	44.6	44.6	44.1	43.8	43.9	43.4	42.9	42.2	43.9
138	Sudan	34.1	–	–	–	–	–	–	–	–	34.1
139	Suriname	39.7	39.8	39.3	38.9	38.1	36.9	36.5	35.9	35.1	37.8
140	Swaziland	43.5	41.4	41.3	40.9	40.2	40.1	39.3	38.9	–	40.7
141	Sweden	19.6	19.2	19.1	19.0	18.7	18.5	18.6	18.2	17.9	18.8
142	Switzerland	8.8	8.6	8.6	8.6	8.8	8.6	8.5	8.3	8.1	8.5
143	Syrian Arab Republic	19.3	19.3	19.2	19.1	19.3	19.1	19.0	18.7	18.5	19.1
144	Taiwan	25.7	25.4	25.7	25.4	25.2	24.7	24.5	24.2	23.9	25.0
145	Tajikistan	43.5	43.2	42.9	42.7	42.1	41.7	41.5	41.2	41.0	42.2
146	Tanzania	58.6	58.3	57.7	56.9	56.6	56.0	55.4	54.7	53.7	56.4
147	Thailand	53.4	52.6	52.4	51.5	50.2	49.6	49.0	48.5	48.2	50.6
148	Togo	34.4	35.1	35.4	34.5	34.9	35.0	35.0	34.6	–	34.9

No.	Country	Years									Country average
		1999	2000	2001	2002	2003	2004	2005	2006	2007	
149	Trinidad and Tobago	34.7	34.4	34.3	34.4	33.4	33.1	32.9	31.9	31.5	33.4
150	Tunisia	38.7	38.4	37.8	37.8	37.4	36.9	36.7	35.9	35.4	37.2
151	Turkey	32.7	32.1	32.8	32.4	31.8	31.0	30.0	29.5	29.1	31.3
152	Uganda	43.5	43.1	42.9	42.9	42.5	42.4	42.2	41.0	40.3	42.3
153	Ukraine	52.7	52.2	51.4	50.8	49.7	48.8	47.8	47.3	46.8	49.7
154	United Arab Emirates	26.3	26.4	27.0	27.4	26.3	25.4	24.8	23.5	–	25.9
155	United Kingdom	12.8	12.7	12.6	12.6	12.5	12.4	12.4	12.3	12.2	12.5
156	United States	8.8	8.7	8.8	8.8	8.7	8.6	8.5	8.4	8.4	8.6
157	Uruguay	50.5	51.1	51.7	54.0	53.6	51.1	49.2	48.5	46.1	50.6
158	Venezuela, RB	33.8	33.6	33.5	35.5	36.9	34.9	33.5	32.0	30.9	33.8
159	Vietnam	15.8	15.6	15.5	15.3	15.2	15.1	14.7	14.6	14.4	15.1
160	Yemen, Rep.	27.7	27.4	27.3	27.2	27.0	27.0	26.6	26.8	26.8	27.1
161	Zambia	49.3	48.9	48.3	48.1	47.5	46.8	46.3	45.0	43.9	47.1
162	Zimbabwe	59.6	59.4	61.5	62.8	63.7	62.3	62.0	62.3	62.7	61.8
	Time average	34.0	33.7	33.6	33.6	33.3	32.9	32.5	32.1	31.2	

Source: Bühn, Montenegro and Schneider (2010), pp. 455–61

REFERENCES

Adams, C. and P. Webley (2001), 'Small business owners' attitudes on VAT compliance in the UK', *Journal of Economic Psychology*, 22(2): 195–216.

Adjerad, S. (2003), *Dynamisme du Secteur des Emplois Familiales en 2002*, Paris: DARES Premières Informations.

Alderslade, J., J. Talmage and Y. Freeman (2006), 'Measuring the informal economy: one neighborhood at a time', Discussion Paper, Brookings Institution Metropolitan Policy Program, Washington, DC, September.

Allingham, M. G. and A. Sandmo (1972), 'Income tax evasion: a theoretical analysis', *Journal of Public Economics*, 1(3): 323–38.

Alm, J. and B. Torgler (2006), 'Culture differences and tax morale in the United States and in Europe', *Journal of Economic Psychology*, 27(2): 224–46.

Alm, J., I. Sanchez and A. de Juan (1995), 'Economic and non-economic factors in tax compliance', *Kyklos*, 48: 3–18.

Andreoni, J., B. Erard and J. Feinstein (1998), 'Tax compliance', *Journal of Economic Literature*, 36(4): 818–60.

Ayres, I. and V. Braithwaite (1992), *Responsive Regulation: Transcending the deregulation debate*, Oxford: Oxford University Press.

Bàculo, L. (2001), 'The shadow economy in Italy: results from field studies', Paper presented at the European Scientific Workshop on 'The shadow economy: empirical evidence and new policy issues at the European level', Ragusa, Sicily, 20–21 September.

Bàculo, L. (2002), 'The shadow economy in Italy', Paper presented at conference on 'Unofficial activities in transition countries: ten years of experience', Zagreb.

Bàculo, L. (2003), 'Valutazione di una politica per l'emersione: i contratti di riallineamento', *Rassegna italiana di valutazione*, 26.

Bàculo, L. (2005), 'Harnessing entrepreneurship in the shadow economy: the Naples CUORE experiment', Paper presented at the Public Administration Committee Conference, University of Nottingham, Nottingham, September.

Bàculo, L. (2006), 'Tackling informal employment: the case of southern Italy', *International Journal of Manpower*, 27: 552–71.

Bajada, C. and F. Schneider (2005), *Size, Causes and Consequences of the Underground Economy: An International Perspective*, Aldershot: Ashgate.

Bajada, C. and F. Schneider (2009), 'Unemployment and the shadow economy in the OECD', *Review Economique*, 60(4): 1011–33.

Balkin, S. (1989), *Self-Employment for Low-Income People*, New York: Praeger.

Bartlett, B. (1998), 'Corruption, the Underground Economy, and Taxation', unpublished manuscript, National Center for Policy Analysis, Washington, DC.

Bergman, M. and A. Nevarez (2006), 'Do audits enhance compliance? An empirical assessment of VAT enforcement', *National Tax Journal*, 59(4): 817–32.

Beron, K. J., H. V. Tauchen and A. D. Witte (1992), 'The effect of audits and socio-economic variables on compliance', in J. Slemrod (ed.), *Why People Pay Taxes*, Ann Arbor: University of Michigan Press, pp. 67–89.

Bhattacharyya, D. K. (1990), 'An econometric method of estimating the hidden economy, United Kingdom (1960–1984): estimates and tests', *Economic Journal*, 100: 703–17.

Bhattacharyya, D. K. (1999), 'On the economic rationale of estimating the hidden economy', *Economic Journal*, 109(3): 348–59.

Bird, R. M. and E. M. Zolt (2008), 'Tax policy in emerging countries', *Environment and Planning C*, 26(1): 73–86.

Blackwell, C. (2009), 'A meta-analysis of incentive effects in tax compliance experiments', in J. Alm, J. Martinez-Vazquez and B. Torgler (eds), *Developing Alternative Frameworks Explaining Tax Compliance*, London: Routledge, pp. 164–81.

Blackwell, C. (2010), 'A meta analysis of incentive effects, Intex compliance experiments', in J. Alm, J. Martinez-Vazquez and B. Torgler (eds), *Developing Alternative Frameworks Explaining Tax Compliance*, London: Routledge.

Blumenthal, M., C. Christian and J. Slemrod (1998), *The Determinants of Income Tax Compliance: Evidence from a controlled experiment in Minnesota*, Working Paper 6575, Massachusetts: National Bureau of Economic Research.

Blumenthal, M., C. Christian and J. Slemrod (2001), 'Do normative appeals affect tax compliance? Evidence from a controlled experiment in Minnesota', *National Tax Journal*, 54(1): 125–36.

Braithwaite, J. (2002), *Restorative Justice and Responsive Regulation*, Oxford: Oxford University Press.

Braithwaite, V. (2007), 'Responsive regulation and taxation: introduction', *Law and Policy*, 29(1): 3–10.

Braithwaite, V. and M. Reinhart (2000), *The Taxpayers' Charter: does the Australian Tax Office comply and who benefits?*, Centre for Tax System Integrity Working Paper no. 1, Australian National University, Canberra.

Breusch, T. (2005a), 'The Canadian underground economy: an examination of Giles and Tedds', *Canadian Tax Journal*, 53(4): 367–91.

Breusch, T. (2005b), 'Estimating the underground economy using MIMIC models', Working Paper, Canberra, Australia, http://econwpa.wustl.edu/eps/em/papers/0507/0507003.pdf.

Brück, T., J. B. Haisten-DeNew and K. F. Zimmermann (2006), 'Creating low-skilled jobs by subsidizing market contracted household work', *Applied Economics*, 38(4): 899–911.

Bühn, A. and F. Schneider (2011), 'Corruption and the shadow economy: like oil and vinegar, like water and fire?', *International Tax and Public Finance*, LLC: 220–41.

Bühn, A., A. Karmann and F. Schneider (2009), 'Shadow economy and do-it-yourself activities: the German case', *Journal of Institutional and Theoretical Economics*, 165(4): 701–22.

Bühn, A., C. Montenegro and F. Schneider (2010), 'New estimates for the shadow economies all over the world', *International Economic Journal*, 24(4): 443–61.

Caianiello, D. and I. Voltura (2003), *Proposal for a Service Bureau*, Rome: Comitato per l'emersione del lavoro no regolare.

Capital Economics Ltd (2003), *VAT and the Construction Industry*, London: Capital Economics Ltd.

Cappiello, M. A. (1986), 'Proposita di bibliografia ragionata sull'economia sommersa nell'industria (Italia 1970–82)', in A. Bagnasco (ed.), *L'altra metà dell'economia, La ricerca internazionale sull'economia informale*, Naples: Liguori, pp. 307–45.

Carroll, J. (1987), 'Compliance with the law: a decision-making approach to taxpaying', *Law and Human Behavior*, 11: 319–35.

Centre for Economic and Social Inclusion (2006), *Evaluation of the Hartlepool 'informal to formal' pilot*, Manchester: Centre for Economic and Social Inclusion.

Chang, J. J. and C. C. Lai (2004), 'Collaborative tax evasion and social norms: why deterrence does not work', *Oxford Economic Papers*, 56(2): 244–68.

Charmes, J. (2000), 'Informal sector poverty and gender, a review of the empirical evidence', paper prepared on behalf of Wiego (Women in Informal Employment: Globalizing and Organizing), Washington, DC, and Paris: OECD and World Bank.

Chen, M. (2004), 'Rethinking the informal economy: linkages with the formal economy and the formal regulatory environment', paper presented at the EGDI-WIDR conference 'Unleashing human potential: linking the informal and formal sectors', Helsinki, Finland.

Chickering, L. A. and M. Salahdine (eds) (1991), *The Silent Revolution – the Informal Sector in Five Asian and Near Eastern*

Countries, An International Center for Economic Growth Publication, San Francisco: ICS Press.

Chittenden, F., S. Kauser and P. Poutzouris (2002), *Regulatory Burdens of Small Business: A literature review,* www.berr.gov.uk/files/file38324.pdf.

Chittenden, F., S. Kauser and P. Poutzouris (2003), 'Tax regulation and small business in the USA, UK, Australia and New Zealand', *International Small Business Journal,* 21(1): 93–115.

Chung, J. and V. U. Trivedi (2003), 'The effect of friendly persuasion and gender on tax compliance behaviour', *Journal of Business Ethics,* 47(2): 133–45.

Comitato per l'emersione del lavoro no regolare (2003), 'The Figure of the National Committee, the Provincial and Regional Commissions, and the tutors for the surfacing of undeclared work', Rome: Comitato per l'emersione del lavoro no regolare.

Copisarow, R. (2004), 'Street UK – a micro-finance organisation: lessons learned from its first three years' operations', Birmingham: Street UK.

Copisarow, R. and A. Barbour (2004), *Self-Employed People in the Informal Economy: Cheats or contributors?,* London: Community Links.

Cullis, J. G. and A. Lewis (1997), 'Why people pay taxes: from a conventional economic model to a model of social convention', *Journal of Economic Psychology,* 18(2/3): 305–21.

Dallago, B. (1990), *The Irregular Economy: The 'Underground Economy' and the 'Black Labor Market',* Dartmouth, UK: Ashgate.

Davis, J. S., G. Hecht and J. D. Perkins (2003), 'Social behaviors, enforcement and tax compliance dynamics', *Accounting Review*, 78(1): 39–69.

De Grazia, R. (1983), *Le travail clandestin: Situation dans les pays industrialisés à économie de marché*, Geneva: Bit.

De Juan, A., M. A. Lasheras and R. Mayo (1994), 'Voluntary tax compliant behavior of Spanish income tax payers', *Public Finance*, 49: 90–105.

De Soto, H. (2000), *The Mystery of Capital: Why capitalism triumphs in the West and fails everywhere else*, London: Black Swan.

Dekker, H., E. Oranje, P. Renooy, F. Rosing and C. C. Williams (2010), 'Joining up the fight against undeclared work in the European Union', Brussels: DG Employment, Social Affairs and Equal Opportunities, http://ec.europa.eu/social/main.jsp?catId=471&langId=en.

Dell'Anno, R. (2003), 'Estimating the shadow economy in Italy: a structural equation approach', Working Paper 2003–7, Department of Economics, University of Aarhus.

Dell'Anno, R. and F. Schneider (2003), 'The shadow economy of Italy and other OECD countries: what do we know?', *Journal of Public Finance and Public Choice*, 21: 223–45.

Dell'Anno, R. and F. Schneider (2009), 'A complex approach to estimate shadow economy: the structural equation modelling', in M. Faggnini and T. Looks (eds), *Coping with the Complexity of Economics*, Berlin: Springer, pp. 110–30.

Deregulierungskommission (Deregulation Commission) (1991), 'Opening of markets and competition', Report 4378, presented to the German Federal Government, Bonn.

Dixon, H. (1999), 'Controversy, on the hidden economy, editorial introduction', *Economic Journal*, 456(3): 335–7.

Dreher, A. and F. Schneider (2009), 'Corruption and the shadow economy: an empirical analysis', *Public Choice*, 144(2): 215–77.

Dreher, A., C. Kotsogiannis and S. McCorriston (2007), 'Corruption around the world: evidence from a structural model', *Journal of Comparative Economics*, 35(4): 443–66.

Dreher, A., C. Kotsogiannis and S. McCorriston (2009), 'How do institutions affect corruption and the shadow economy?', *International Tax and Public Finance*, 16(4): 773–96.

Dubin, J. A. and L. L. Wilde (1988), 'An empirical analysis of federal income tax auditing and compliance', *National Tax Journal*, 41: 61–74.

Dubin, J. A., M. J. Graetz and L. L. Wilde (1987), 'Are we a nation of tax cheaters? New econometric evidence on tax compliance', *American Economic Review*, 77: 240–45.

Elffers, H. and D. J. Hessing (1997), 'Influencing the prospects of tax evasion', *Journal of Economic Psychology*, 18: 289–304.

Elffers, H., R. H. Wiegal and D. J. Hessing (1987), 'The consequences of different strategies for measuring tax evasion behaviour', *Journal of Economic Psychology*, 8: 311–37.

Enste, D. and F. Schneider (2006), 'Umfang und Entwicklung der Schattenwirtschaft in 145 Ländern', in F. Schneider and D. Enste (eds), *Jahrbuch Schattenwirtschaft 2006/07. Zum Spannungsfeld von Poltik und Ökonomie*, Berlin: LIT Verlag, pp. 55–80.

Etzioni, A. (1988), *The Moral Dimension*, New York: Free Press.

European Commission (2007), 'Stepping up the fight against undeclared work', COM(2007) 628 final, Brussels: European Commission.

European Parliament Committee on Employment and Social Affairs (2008), *Draft Report on Stepping up the Fight against Undeclared Work*, 2008/2035(INI), Brussels: European Parliament Committee on Employment and Social Affairs.

Evans, M., S. Syrett and C. C. Williams (2006), *Informal Economic Activities and Deprived Neighbourhoods*, London: Department of Communities and Local Government.

Falkinger, J. (1988), 'Tax evasion and equity: a theoretical analysis', *Public Finance*, 43(2): 388–95.

Fehr, E. and B. Rokenbach (2003), 'Detrimental effects of sanctions on human altruism', *Nature*, 422: 137–40.

Feige, E. L. (ed.) (1989), *The Underground Economies. Tax Evasion and Information Distortion*, Cambridge: Cambridge University Press.

Feige, E. L. (1990), 'Defining and estimating underground and informal economies', *World Development*, 18(7): 989–1002.

Feige, E. L. (1994), 'The underground economy and the currency enigma', Supplement to *Public Finance/Finances Publiques*, 49: 119–36.

Feld, L. P. and B. S. Frey (2002a), 'Trust breeds trust: how taxpayers are treated', *Economics of Governments*, 3: 87–99.

Feld, L. P. and B. S. Frey (2002b), 'The tax authority and the taxpayer: an exploratory analysis', Discussion paper, University of Zurich.

Feld, L. P. and B. S. Frey (2007), 'Tax compliance as the result of a psychological tax contract: the role of incentives and responsive regulation', *Law and Policy*, 29(1): 102–20.

Feld, L. P. and C. Larsen (2005), *Black Activities in Germany in 2001 and 2004: A Comparison Based on Survey Data*, Study no. 12, Copenhagen: Rockwool Foundation Research Unit.

Feld, L. P. and C. Larsen (2008), '"Black" activities low in Germany in 2006', *News from the Rockwool Foundation Research Unit*, March, pp. 1–12.

Feld, L. P. and C. Larsen (2009), *Undeclared Work in Germany 2001–2007 – Impact of Deterrence, Tax Policy, and Social Norms: An Analysis Based on Survey Data*, Berlin: Springer.

Feld, L. P., A. Schmidt and F. Schneider (2007), 'Tax evasion, black activities and deterrence in Germany: an institutional and empirical perspective', Discussion paper, Department of Economics, University of Heidelberg, Germany.

Feld, L. P. and F. Schneider (2010), 'Survey on the shadow economy and undeclared earnings in OECD countries', *German Economic Review*, 11(2): 109–49.

Flaming, D., B. Hayolamak and P. Jossart (2005), *Hopeful Workers, Marginal Jobs: LA's Off-the-Books Labor Force*, Los Angeles, CA: Economic Roundtable.

Fleming, M. H., J. Roman and G. Farrel (2000), 'The shadow economy', *Journal of International Affairs*, 53(2): 64–89.

Frey, B. (1997a), 'A constitution for knaves crowds out civic virtue', *Economic Journal*, 107: 1043–53.

Frey, B. S. (1997b), *Not Just for the Money: An Economic Theory of Personal Motivation*, Cheltenham: Edward Elgar.

Frey, B. S. and W. Pommerehne (1984), 'The hidden economy: state and prospect for measurement', *Review of Income and Wealth*, 30(1): 1–23.

Frey, B. S. and H. Weck (1983), 'What produces a hidden economy? An international cross-section analysis', *Southern Economic Journal*, 49(4): 822–32.

Frey, B. S. and H. Weck-Hannemann (1984), 'The hidden economy an "unobserved" variable', *European Economic Review*, 26: 33–53.

Frey, L. (1972), *Il lavoro a domicilio in Lombardia, Giunta Regionale Lombarda*, Milan: Assessorato al Lavoro.

Frey, L. (1975), 'Il potenziale di lavoro in Italia', Documenti ISVET no. 50.

Frey, L. (1978), 'Il lavoro nero nel 1977 in Italia', Tendenze della occupazione no. 6.

Frey, L. (1980), 'Introduzione all'analisi economica del lavoro minorile', *Economia del Lavoro*, 1/2: 5–16.

Friedland, N. (1982), 'A note on tax evasion as a function of the quality of information about the magnitude and credibility of threatened fines: some preliminary research', *Journal of Applied Social Psychology*, 12: 54–9.

Friedland, N., S. Maital and A. Rutenberg (1978), 'A simulation study of income tax evasion', *Journal of Public Economics*, 10: 107–16.

Friedman, E., S. Johnson, D. Kaufmann and P. Zoido-Lobatón (2000), 'Dodging the grabbing hand: the determinants of unofficial activity in 69 countries', *Journal of Public Economics*, 76(4): 459–93.

Gaetani-d'Aragona, G. (1979), 'I sommersi', *Nord e Sud*, 7: 26–46.

Gallin, D. (2001), 'Propositions on trade unions and informal employment in time of globalization', *Antipode*, 19(4): 531–49.

Ghezzi, S. (2009), 'The fallacy of the formal and informal divide: lessons from a post-Fordist regional economy', in E. Marcelli, C.C. Williams and P. Joassart (eds), *Informal Work in Developed Nations*, London: Routledge.

Giles, D. E. A. (1999a), 'Measuring the hidden economy: implications for econometric modelling', *Economic Journal*, 109(3): 370–80.

Giles, D. E. A. (1999b), 'Modelling the hidden economy in the tax-gap in New Zealand', *Empirical Economics*, 24(4): 621–40.

Giles, D. E. A. (1999c), 'The rise and fall of the New Zealand underground economy: are the reasons symmetric?', *Applied Economic Letters*, 6: 185–9.

Giles, D. E. A. and L. M. Tedds (2002), 'Taxes and the Canadian underground economy', Canadian Tax Paper no. 106, Canadian Tax Foundation, Toronto/Ontario.

Grabiner, Lord (2000), *The Informal Economy*, London: HM Treasury.

Haigner, S., S. Jenewein, F. Schneider and F. Wakolbinger (2011), 'Dissatisfaction, fear and annoyance: driving forces of informal labor supply and demand', Discussion paper, Department of Economics, University of Linz, Linz, Austria. Paper presented at the European Public Choice Meeting, Rennes, 28 April–1 May.

Hansford, A., J. Hasseldine and C. Howorth (2003), 'Factors affecting the costs of UK VAT compliance for small and medium-sized enterprises', *Environment and Planning C*, 21(4): 479–92.

Hart, M., R. Blackburn and J. Kitching (2005), *The Impact of Regulation on Small Business Growth: An outline research programme*, London: Small Business Research Centre, Kingston University.

Hasseldine, J. (1998), 'Tax amnesties: an international review', *Bulletin for International Fiscal Documentation*, 52(7): 303–10.

Hasseldine, J. and Z. Li (1999), 'More tax evasion research required in new millennium', *Crime, Law and Social Change*, 31(1): 91–104.

Hasseldine, J., P. Hite, S. James and M. Toumi (2007), 'Persuasive communications: tax compliance enforcement strategies for sole proprietors', *Contemporary Accounting Research*, 24(1): 171–84.

Hazans, M. (2011), 'Informal workers across Europe, evidence from 30 countries', Discussion and background paper, World Bank P112988, University of Latvia.

Heintz, E. and G. B. Chang (2007), *Report of Informal Employment for the ILO*, Geneva: ILO.

Herwartz, H., F. Schneider and E. Tafenau (2009), 'One share fits it all? Regional variation in the shadow economy in the EU regions', Discussion paper, Universities of Linz and Kiel.

Hvidtfeldt, C., B. Jensen and C. Larsen (2011), 'Undeclared work and the Danes', University Press of Southern Denmark, June. English summary reported in: *News*, Rockwool Foundation Research Unit, March, Copenhagen, Denmark.

IfD Allensbach (1975), *Studie im Auftrag der Kommission für Wirtschaftlichen und Sozialen Wandel*, Bodensee: Allensbach.

ILO (2002), *Decent Work and the Informal Economy*, Geneva: International Labour Organisation.

Isachsen, A. J. and S. Strøm (1985), 'The size and growth of the hidden economy in Norway', *Review of Income and Wealth*, 31(1): 21–38.

Jensen, L., G. T. Cornwell and J. L. Findeis (1995), 'Informal work in nonmetropolitan Pennsylvania', *Rural Sociology*, 60(1): 91–107.

Job, J., A. Stout and R. Smith (2007), 'Culture change in three taxation administrations: from command-and-control to responsive regulation', *Law and Policy*, 29: 84–101.

Johnson, S., D. Kaufmann and A. Shleifer (1997), 'The unofficial economy in transition', Brookings Papers on Economic Activity no. 2, pp. 159–221.

Johnson, S., D. Kaufmann and P. Zoido-Lobatón (1998a), 'Regulatory discretion and the unofficial economy', *American Economic Review, Papers and Proceedings*, 88(2): 387–92.

Johnson, S., D. Kaufmann and P. Zoido-Lobatón (1998b), 'Corruption, public finances and the unofficial economy', World Bank Policy Research Working Paper Series no. 2169, Washington, DC: World Bank.

Jurik, N. C. (2005), *Bootstrap Dreams: U.S. microenterprise development in an era of welfare reform*, Ithaca, NY: Cornell University Press.

Kagan, A. and T. Scholz (1984), 'The criminology of the corporation and regulatory enforcement strategies', in K. Hawkins and J. M. Thomas (eds), *Enforcing Regulation*, Boston, MA: Kluwer Nijhoff.

Kanniainen, V., J. Pääkönen and F. Schneider (2004), 'Fiscal and ethical determinants of shadow economy: theory and evidence', Discussion paper, Department of Economics, Johannes Kepler University of Linz, Linz, Austria.

Karmann, A. (1986), 'Monetäre Ansätze zur Erfassung der Schattenwirtschaft: Ein Vergleich verschiedener Messansätze', *Kredit und Kapitel*, 19: 233–47.

Karmann, A. (1990), 'Schattenwirtschaft und ihre Ursachen: Eine empirische Analyse zur Schwarzwirtschaft und Selbstversorgung in der Bundesrepublik Deutschland',

Zeitschrift für Wirtschafts- und Sozialwissenschaften (ZWS), 110: 185–206.

Kastlunger, B., E. Kirchler, L. Mittore and J. Pitters (2009), 'Sequences of audits, tax compliance, and taxpaying strategies', *Journal of Economic Psychology*, 30(4): 405–18.

Kazemier, B. (2005a), 'The underground economy: a survey of methods and estimates', Discussion paper, Voorburg: Statistics Netherlands.

Kazemier, B. (2005b), 'Monitoring the underground labour market: what surveys can do', Discussion paper, Voorburg: Statistics Netherlands.

Kazemier, B. (2006), 'Monitoring the underground economy: a survey of methods and estimates', in F. Schneider and D. Enste (eds), *Jahrbuch Schattenwirtschaft 2006/07. Zum Spannungsfeld von Politik und Ökonomie*, Berlin: LIT Verlag, pp. 11–53.

Kinsey, K. (1992), 'Deterrence and alienation effects of IRS enforcement: an analysis of survey data', in J. Slemrod (ed.), *Why People Pay Taxes*, Michigan: University of Michigan Press.

Kinsey, K. and H. Gramsick (1993), 'Did the Tax Reform Act of 1986 improve compliance? Three studies of pre- and post-TRA compliance attitudes', *Law and Policy*, 15: 293–325.

Kinsey, K., H. Gramsick and K. Smith (1991), 'Framing justice: taxpayer evaluations of personal tax burdens', *Law and Society Review*, 25: 845–73.

Kirchgässner, G. (1983), 'Size and development of the West German shadow economy, 1955–1980', *Zeitschrift für die gesamte Staatswissenschaft* (ZgS)/*Journal of Institutional and Theoretical Economics* (JITE), 139: 197–214.

Kirchgässner, G. (1984), 'Verfahren zur Erfassung des in der Schattenwirtschaft erarbeiteten Sozialprodukts', *Allgemeines Statistisches Archiv*, 68: 378–405.

Kirchler, E. (2007), *The Economic Psychology of Tax Behaviour*, Cambridge: Cambridge University Press.

Kirchler, E., E. Hoelzl and I. Wahl (2007), 'Enforced versus voluntary tax compliance: the "slippery slope" framework', *Journal of Economic Psychology*, 29(2): 210–25.

Kirchler, E., B. Maciejovsky and F. Schneider (2003) 'Everyday representations of tax avoidance, tax evasion and tax flight: do legal differences matter?', *Journal of Economic Psychology*, 24(4): 535–53.

Klepper, S. and D. Nagin (1989), 'Tax compliance and perceptions of the risks of detection and criminal prosecution', *Law and Society Review*, 23: 209–40.

Kopp, R. J., W. W. Pommerehne and N. Schwarz (1997), *Determining the Value of Non-Marketed Goods: Economic, Psychological, and Policy Relevant Aspects of Contingent Valuation Methods*, Boston, MA: Kluwer Academic Publishing.

Körner, M., H. Strotmann, L. P. Feld and F. Schneider (2006), 'Steuermoral – das Spannungsfeld von Freiwilligkeit der Steuerhinterziehung und Regelverstoë durch Steuerhinterzierung', IAW Forschungsbereicht no. 64, Tübingen.

Kornhauser, M. E. (2008), 'Normative and cognitive aspects of tax compliance: literature review and recommendations for the IRS regarding individual taxpayers', Washington, DC: Internal Revenue Service.

Kucera, D. and L. Roncolato (2008), 'Informal employment: two contested policy issues', *International Labor Review*, 147(4): 321–48.

Langfeldt, E. (1984a), 'The unobserved economy in the Federal Republic of Germany', in. E. L. Feige (ed.), *The Unobserved Economy*, Cambridge: Cambridge University Press, pp. 236–60.

Langfeldt, E. (1984b), *Die Schattenwirtschaft in der Bundesrepublik Deutschland*, Kieler Studien 191, Tübingen: Mohr Siebeck Verlag.

Le Feuvre, N. (2000), *Employment, Family and Community Activities: A new balance for men and women – summary of the French national report*, Dublin: European Foundation for the Improvement of Living and Working Conditions.

Lemieux, T., B. Fortin and P. Fréchette (1994), 'The effect of taxes on labor supply in the underground economy', *American Economic Review*, 84(3): 231–54.

Leonard, M. (1998), *Invisible Work, Invisible Workers: The informal economy in Europe and the US*, London: Macmillan.

Lippert, O. and M. Walker (eds) (1997), *The Underground Economy: Global Evidences of its Size and Impact*, Vancouver, BC: Frazer Insitute.

Loayza, N. V. (1996), 'The economics of the informal sector: a simple model and some empirical evidence from Latin America', *Carnegie-Rochester Conference Series on Public Policy*, 45: 129–62.

Loayza, N. V., A. M. Oviedo and L. Servén (2005a), 'The impact of regulation on growth and informality: cross country evidence', Policy Research Paper WPS3623, Washington, DC: World Bank.

Loayza, N. V., A. M. Oviedo and L. Servén (2005b), 'Regulation and firm dynamics', Discussion paper, Washington, DC: World Bank.

López Laborda, J. and F. Rodrigo (2003), 'Tax amnesties and income tax compliance: the case of Spain', *Fiscal Studies*, 24(1): 73–96.

Lubell, H. (1991), *The Informal Sector in the 1980s and 1990s*, Paris: OECD.

Macafee, K. (1980), 'A glimpse of the hidden economy in the national accounts', *Economic Trends*, 2(1): 81–7.

Marcelli, E. A. (2004), 'Unauthorized Mexican immigration, the labour and other lower-wage informal employment in California', *Regional Studies*, 38(1): 1–13.

Marcelli, E. A., M. Pastor, Jr, and P. M. Joassart (1999), 'Estimating the effects of informal economic activity: evidence from Los Angeles County', *Journal of Economic Issues*, 33: 579–607.

Mason, R. and L. Calvin (1984), 'Public confidence and admitted tax evasion', *National Tax Journal*, 37(4): 489–96.

Matthews, K. and J. Lloyd-Williams (2001), 'The VAT evading firm and VAT evasion: an empirical analysis', *International Journal of the Economics of Business*, 6(1): 39–50.

McBarnet, D. (2003), 'When compliance is not the solution but the problem: from changes in law to changes in attitude', in V. Braithwaite (ed.), *Taxing Democracy: Understanding tax avoidance and evasion*, Aldershot: Ashgate.

Meldolesi, L. and S. Ruvolo (2003), *A Project for Formalisation*, Rome: Comitato per l'emersione del lavoro no regolare.

Merz, J. and K. G. Wolff (1993), 'The shadow economy: illicit work and household production – a microanalysis of West Germany', *Review of Income and Wealth*, 39(2): 177–94.

Michaelis, C., K. Smith and S. Richards (2001), *Regular Survey of Small Businesses' Opinions: First survey – final report*, www.berr. gov.uk/files/file38259.pdf.

Milliron, V. and D. Toy (1988), 'Tax compliance: an investigation of key features', *Journal of the American Tax Association*, 9(1): 84–104.

Ministero del Lavoro, della Salute e delle Politiche Sociali (2008), *Rapporto di monitoraggio delle politiche occupazionali e del lavoro*, Rome: Ministero del Lavoro, della Salute e delle Politiche Sociali.

Mogensen, G. V. (1985) *Sort Arbejde i Danmark*, Copenhagen: Institut for Nationalokonomi.

Mogensen, G. V., H. K. Kvist, E. Körmendi and S. Pedersen (1995), *The Shadow Economy in Demark 1994: Measurement and Results*, Study no. 3, Copenhagen: Rockwool Foundation Research Unit.

Mummert, A. and F. Schneider (2001), 'The German shadow economy: parted in a united Germany?', *Finanzarchiv*, 58: 260–85.

Murphy, K. (2005), 'Regulating more effectively: the relationship between procedural justice, legitimacy and tax non-compliance', *Journal of Law and Society*, 32(4): 562–89.

Murphy, K. (2008), 'Enforcing tax compliance: to punish or persuade?', *Economic Analysis and Policy*, 38(1): 113–35.

Murphy, K. and N. Harris (2007), 'Shaming, shame and recidivism: a test of re-integrative shaming theory in the white-collar crime context', *British Journal of Criminology*, 47: 900–917.

NAO (National Audit Office) (2008), *Tackling the Hidden Economy*, London: National Audit Office.

OECD (2000), *Tax Avoidance and Evasion*, Paris: OECD.

OECD (2008), 'Declaring work or staying underground: informal employment in 7 OECD countries', *OECD Employment Outlook*, ch. 2, Paris: OECD.

OECD (2009a), *Is Informal Normal? Towards More and Better Jobs in Developing Countries*, Paris: OECD.

OECD (2009b), *Policy Round Tables, Competition Policy and the Informal Economy*, Paris: OECD.

OECD (2010), *Economic Outlook Data Base*, Paris: OECD.

OECD (2011), 'Towards a better understanding of the informal economy', by D. Andrews, A. Caldera Sánchez and A. Johansson, OECD Economics Department Working Papers no. 873, Paris: OECD.

Pahl, R. E. (1984), *Divisions of Labour*, Oxford: Blackwell.

Pedersen, S. (2003), *The Shadow Economy in Germany, Great Britain and Scandinavia: A Measurement Based on Questionnaire Service*, Study no. 10, Copenhagen: Rockwool Foundation Research Unit.

Pickhardt, M. and J. Sardà Pons (2006), 'Size and scope of the underground economy in Germany', *Applied Economics*, 38(4): 1707–13.

Posner, E. A. (2000a), *Law and Social Norms*, Cambridge, MA: Harvard University Press.

Posner, E. A. (2000b), 'Law and social norms: the case of tax compliance', *Virginia Law Review*, 86(6): 1781–1820.

Pozo, S. (ed.) (1996), *Exploring the Underground Economy: Studies of Illegal and Unreported Activity*, Michigan: W. E. Upjohn Institute for Employment Research.

Renooy, P. (1990), *The Informal Economy: Meaning, measurement and social significance*, Netherlands Geographical Studies no. 115, Amsterdam.

Renooy, P., S. Ivarsson, O. van der Wusten-Gritsai and R. Meijer (2004), *Undeclared Work in an Enlarged Union: An analysis of shadow work – an in-depth study of specific items*, Brussels: European Commission.

Riahi-Belkaoui, A. (2004), 'Relationship between tax compliance internationally and selected determinants of tax morale', *Journal of International Accounting, Auditing and Taxation*, 13(2): 135–43.

Richardson, G. (2006), 'Determinants of tax evasion: a cross-country investigation', *Journal of International Accounting, Auditing and Taxation*, 15(2): 150–69.

Richardson, M. and A. Sawyer (2001), 'A taxonomy of the tax compliance literature: further findings, problems and prospects', *Australian Tax Forum*, 16(2): 137–320.

Roth, J. A., J. T. Scholoz and A. D. Witte (1989), *Taxpayer Compliance*, vol. 1: *An Agenda for Research*, Philadelphia: University of Pennsylvania Press.

Ruesga, B. S. M. (1984), 'Economía oculta y mercado de trabajo: aproximación al caso español', *Información commercial espaniola*, pp. 55–61.

Sandford, C. (1999), 'Policies dealing with tax evasion', in E. Feige and K. Ott (eds), *Underground Economies in Transition: Unrecorded activity, tax evasion, corruption and organized crime*, Aldershot: Ashgate.

Schneider, F. (1986), 'Estimating the size of the Danish shadow economy using the currency demand approach: an attempt', *Scandinavian Journal of Economics*, 88(4): 643–68.

Schneider, F. (1994a), 'Measuring the size and development of the shadow economy. Can the causes be found and the obstacles be overcome?', in H. Brandstaetter and W. Güth (eds), *Essays on Economic Psychology*, Berlin: Springer, pp. 193–212.

Schneider, F. (1994b), 'Determinanten der Steuerhinterziehung der Schwarzarbeit im internationalen Vergleich', in C. Smekal and E. Theurl (eds), *Stand und Entwicklung der Finanzpsychologie*, Baden-Baden: Nomos, pp. 247–88.

Schneider, F. (1994c), 'Can the shadow economy be reduced through major tax reforms? An empirical investigation for Austria', Supplement to *Public Finance/Finances Publiques*, 49: 137–152.

Schneider, F. (1997), 'The shadow economies of western Europe', *Economic Affairs*, 17: 42–8.

Schneider, F. (1998a), 'Further empirical results of the size of the shadow economy of 17 OECD countries over time', paper to be presented at the 54th Congress of the IIPF Cordoba, Argentina, and discussion paper, Department of Economics, University of Linz, Linz, Austria.

Schneider, F. (1998b), 'Stellt das Anwachsen der Schwarzarbeit eine wirtschaftspolitische Herausforderung dar? Einige Gedanken aus volkswirtschaftlicher Sicht', *Mitteilungen des Instituts für angewandte Wirtschaftsforschung* (IAW), I(98): 4–13.

Schneider, F. (1999), 'Ist Schwarzarbeit ein Volkssport geworden? Ein internationaler Vergleich des Ausmaēes der Schwarzarbeit von 1970–97', in S. Lamnek and J. Luedtke (eds), *Der Sozialstaat zwischen Markt und Hedeonismus*, Opladen: Leske und Budrich, pp. 126–61.

Schneider, F. (2000), 'The increase of the size of the shadow economy of 18 OECD countries: some preliminary explanations', Paper presented at the Annual Public Choice Meeting, 10–12 March, Charleston, SC.

Schneider, F. (2001), 'Die Schattenwirtschaft – Tatbestand, Ursachen, Auswirkungen', in A. Rauscher (ed.), *Die Arbeitswelt im Wandel*, Cologne: J. P. Bachem, pp. 127–43.

Schneider, F. (2003), 'Shadow economy', in C. K. Rowley and F. Schneider (eds), *Encyclopedia of Public Choice*, vol. II, Dordrecht: Kluwer Academic Publishers, pp. 286–96.

Schneider, F. (2005), 'Shadow economies around the world: what do we really know?', *European Journal of Political Economy*, 21(4): 598–642.

Schneider, F. (2006), 'Shadow economies and corruption all over the world: what do we really know?', Discussion paper, Institut für Volkswirtschaftslehre, University of Linz, Linz, Austria, August.

Schneider, F. (2007), 'Shadow economies and corruption all over the world: new estimates for 145 countries', *Economics*, 2007-9, July.

Schneider, F. (2009), 'Size and development of the shadow economy in Germany, Austria and other OECD countries: some preliminary findings', *Revue Economique*, 60: 1079–1116.

Schneider, F. (2010), 'The influence of public institutions on the shadow economy: an empirical investigation for OECD countries', *European Journal of Law and Economics*, 6(3): 441–68.

Schneider, F. (ed.) (2011), *Handbook on the Shadow Economy*, Cheltenham: Edward Elgar.

Schneider, F. (2012), 'Size and development of the shadow economy of 31 European and 5 other OECD countries from 2003 to 2012: some new facts', http://www.econ. jku.at/members/Schneider/files/publications/2012/ ShadEcEurope31_March 2012.pdf.

Schneider, F., A. Bühn and C. E. Montenegro (2010), 'New estimates for the shadow economies all over the world', *International Economic Journal*, 24(4): 443–61.

Schneider, F. and D. Enste (2000a), *Schattenwirtschaft und Schwarzarbeit – Umfang, Ursachen, Wirkungen und wirtschaftspolitische Empfehlungen*, Munich: Oldenbourg.

Schneider, F. and D. Enste (2000b), 'Shadow economies: size, causes and consequences', *Journal of Economic Literature*, 38(1): 73–110.

Schneider, F. and D. Enste (2002), *The Shadow Economy: Theoretical Approaches, Empirical Studies, and Political Implications*, Cambridge: Cambridge University Press.

Schneider, F. and D. Enste (eds) (2006), *Jahrbuch Schattenwirtschaft 2006/07. Zum Spannungsfeld von Politik und Ökonomie*, Berlin: LIT Verlag.

Schneider, F. and D. Teobaldelli (2012), 'Beyond the veil of ignorance: the influence of direct democracy on the shadow economy', CESifo Working Paper M03749, University of Munich, Munich.

Schneider, F., J. Volkert and S. Caspar (2002), *Schattenwirtschaft und Schwarzarbeit: Beliebt bei vielen – Ein Problem für alle?: Eine Analyse der schattenwirtschaftlichen Aktivitäten in Deutschland (am Beispiel Baden-Württemberg) und mögliche politische Konsequenzen*, Baden-Baden: Nomos.

Scholz, J. and M. Lubell (1998), 'Adaptive political attitudes: duty, trust and fear as monitors of tax policy', *American Journal of Political Science*, 42: 903–20.

Schwartz, R. D. and S. Orleans (1967), 'On legal sanctions', *University of Chicago Law Review*, 34: 282–300.

Slemrod, J., M. Blumenthal and C. W. Christian (2001), 'Taxpayer response to an increased probability of audit: evidence from a controlled experiment in Minnesota', *Journal of Public Economics*, 79: 455–83.

Small Business Council (2004), *Small Business in the Informal Economy: Making the transition to the formal economy*, London: Small Business Council.

Smith, K. (1990), 'Integrating three perspectives on non-compliance: a sequential decision-making model', *Criminal Justice and Behavior*, 17: 350–69.

Smith, K. (1992), 'Reciprocity and fairness: positive incentives for tax compliance', in J. Slemrod (ed.), *Why People Pay Taxes*, Michigan: University of Michigan Press.

Smith, K. and K. Kinsey (1987), 'Understanding taxpayer behaviour: a conceptual framework with implications for research', *Law and Society Review*, 21: 639–63.

Smith, P. (1994), 'Assessing the size of the underground economy: the Canadian statistical pespectives', *Canadian Economic Observer*, Catalogue no. 11–010, pp. 16–33.

Spicer, M. W. and S. B. Lunstedt (1976), 'Understanding tax evasion', *Public Finance*, 31: 295–305.

Tafenau, E., H. Herwartz and F. Schneider (2010), 'Regional estimates for the shadow economy in Europe', *International Economic Journal*, 24(4): 629–36.

Tanzi, V. (1999), 'Uses and abuses of estimates of the underground economy', *Economic Journal*, 109(3): 338–47.

Teobaldelli, D. (2011), 'Federalism and the shadow economy', *Public Choice*, 146(3): 269–89.

Teobaldelli, D. and F. Schneider (2012), 'Beyond the veil of ignorance: the influence of direct democracy on the shadow economy', Discussion Paper 2012/4, Department of Economics, University of Linz, Linz.

Thomas, J. J. (1992), *Informal Economic Activity*, New York: Harvester/Wheatsheaf.

Thomas, J. J. (1999), 'Quantifying the black economy: "measurement without theory" yet again?', *Economic Journal*, 109: 381–9.

Thurman, Q. C., C. St John and L. Riggs (1984), 'Neutralisation and tax evasion: how effective would a moral appeal be in improving compliance to tax laws?', *Law and Policy*, 6(3): 309–27.

Torgler, B. (2002), 'Speaking to theorists and searching for facts: tax morale and tax compliance in experiments', *Journal of Economic Survey*, 16(4): 657–83.

Torgler, B. (2003), 'Tax morale in transition countries', *Post-Communist Economies*, 15(3): 357–82.

Torgler, B. (2007), *Tax Compliance and Tax Morale: A Theoretical and Empirical Analysis*, Cheltenham: Edward Elgar.

Torgler, B. and C. A. Schaltegger (2005), 'Tax amnesties and political participation', *Public Finance Review*, 33(3): 403–31.

Torgler, B. and F. Schneider (2009), 'The impact of tax morale and institutional quality on the shadow economy, *Journal of Economic Psychology*, 30(3): 228–45.

Tyler, T. (1997), 'The psychology of legitimacy: a relational perspective in voluntary deference to authorities', *Personality and Social Psychology Review*, 1(4): 323–45.

Tyler, T. R., L. Sherman, H. Strang, G. Barnes and D. Woods (2007), 'Reintegrative shaming, procedural justice and recidivism: the engagement of offenders' psychological mechanisms in the Canberra RISE Drinking-and-Driving Experiment', *Law and Society Review*, 41: 553–86.

UN (United Nations) (2008), *Non Observed Economy and National Accounts, Survey of National Practices*, Geneva: United Nations.

Van Eck, R. and B. Kazemier (1988), 'Features of the hidden economy in the Netherlands', *Review of Income and Wealth*, 34(3): 251–73.

Varma, K. N. and A. N. Doob (1998), 'Deterring economic crimes: the case of tax evasion', *Canadian Journal of Criminology*, 40: 165–84.

Webley, P. and S. Halstead (1986), 'Tax evasion on the micro: significant stimulations per expedient experiments', *Journal of Interdisciplinary Economics*, 1: 87–100.

Weck-Hannemann, H. (1983), *Schattenwirtschaft: Eine Möglichkeit zur Einschränkung der Öffentlichen Verwaltung? Eine ökonomische Analyse*, Bern: Peter Lang Verlag.

Weigel, R., D. Hessin and H. Elffers (1987), 'Tax evasion research: a critical appraisal and theoretical model', *Journal of Economic Psychology*, 8(2): 215–35.

Wenzel, M. (2002), 'The impact of outcome orientation and justice concerns on tax compliance: the role of taxpayers' identity', *Journal of Applied Psychology*, 87: 639–45.

Wenzel, M. (2004a), 'The social side of sanctions: personal and social norms as moderators of deterrence', *Law and Human Behaviour*, 28(5): 547–67.

Wenzel, M. (2004b), 'An analysis of norm processes in tax compliance', *Journal of Economic Psychology*, 25(2): 213–28.

Wenzel, M. (2005a), 'Motivation or rationalisation? Causal relations between ethics, norms and tax compliance', *Journal of Economic Psychology*, 26(4): 491–508.

Wenzel, M. (2005b), 'Misperceptions of social norms about tax compliance: from theory to intervention', *Journal of Economic Psychology*, 26(6): 862–83.

Williams, C. C. (2001), 'Tackling the participation of the unemployed in paid informal work: a critical evaluation of the deterrence approach', *Environment and Planning C*, 19(5): 729–49.

Williams, C. C. (2004a), *Cash-in-Hand Work: The underground sector and the hidden economy of favours*, Basingstoke: Palgrave Macmillan.

Williams, C. C. (2004b), 'Evaluating the architecture of governance in the UK for tackling undeclared work', *Local Governance*, 30(4): 167–77.

Williams, C. C. (2004c), 'Beyond deterrence: rethinking the UK public policy approach towards undeclared work', *Public Policy and Administration*, 19(1): 15–30.

Williams, C. C. (2004d), 'Harnessing enterprise and entrepreneurship in the underground economy', *International Journal of Economic Development*, 6(1): 23–53.

Williams, C. C. (2005), *Small Business in the Informal Economy: Making the transition to the formal economy – the evidence base*, London: Small Business Service.

Williams, C. C. (2006), *The Hidden Enterprise Culture: Entrepreneurship in the underground economy*, Cheltenham: Edward Elgar.

Williams, C. C. (2007), 'Small businesses and the informal economy: evidence from the UK', *International Journal of Entrepreneurial Behaviour and Research*, 13(6): 349–66.

Williams, C. C. (2008), 'Beyond ideal-type depictions of entrepreneurship: some lessons from the service sector in England', *Service Industries Journal*, 28(7/8): 1041–53.

Williams, C. C. (2010a), 'Evaluating the nature of undeclared work in south-eastern Europe', *Employee Relations*, 32(3): 212–26.

Williams, C. C. (2010b), 'Special variations in the hidden enterprise culture: some lessons from England', *Entrepreneurship and Regional Development*, 22(5): 403–23.

Williams, C. C. (2011a), 'A critical evaluation of competing representations of informal employment: some lessons from England', *Review of Social Economy*, 69(2): 211–37.

Williams, C. C. (2011b), 'Reconceptualising men's and women's undeclared work: evidence from Europe', *Gender Work and Organization*, 18(4): 415–37.

Williams, C. C. and S. Nadin (2012), 'Tackling the hidden enterprise culture: government policies to support the formalization of informal entrepreneurship', *Entrepreneurship and Regional Development*, 24(9/10): 895–915.

Williams, C. C. and S. Nadin (2013), 'Evaluating the participation of the unemployed in undeclared work: evidence from a 27 nation European survey', *European Societies*, forthcoming.

Williams, C. C. and P. Renooy (2007), *Tackling Undeclared Work in the European Union*, Dublin: European Foundation for the Improvement of Living and Working Conditions.

Williams, C. C. and P. Renooy (2009), *Measures to Combat Undeclared Work in 27 European Union Member States and Norway*, Dublin: European Foundation for the Improvement of Living and Working Conditions.

Williams, C. C. and J. Windebank (1998), *Informal Employment in the Advanced Economies: Implication for Work and Welfare*, London: Routledge.

Williams, C. C. and J. Windebank (2001a), 'Beyond profit motivated exchange: some lessons from the study of paid informal work', *European Urban and Regional Studies*, 8: 49–61.

Williams, C. C. and J. Windebank (2001b), 'Reconceptualizing paid informal exchange: some lessons from English cities', *Environment and Planning A*, 33: 121–40.

ABOUT THE IEA

The Institute is a research and educational charity (No. CC 235 351), limited by guarantee. Its mission is to improve understanding of the fundamental institutions of a free society by analysing and expounding the role of markets in solving economic and social problems.

The IEA achieves its mission by:

- a high-quality publishing programme
- conferences, seminars, lectures and other events
- outreach to school and college students
- brokering media introductions and appearances

The IEA, which was established in 1955 by the late Sir Antony Fisher, is an educational charity, not a political organisation. It is independent of any political party or group and does not carry on activities intended to affect support for any political party or candidate in any election or referendum, or at any other time. It is financed by sales of publications, conference fees and voluntary donations.

In addition to its main series of publications the IEA also publishes a termly journal, *Economic Affairs*.

The IEA is aided in its work by a distinguished international Academic Advisory Council and an eminent panel of Honorary Fellows. Together with other academics, they review prospective IEA publications, their comments being passed on anonymously to authors. All IEA papers are therefore subject to the same rigorous independent refereeing process as used by leading academic journals.

IEA publications enjoy widespread classroom use and course adoptions in schools and universities. They are also sold throughout the world and often translated/reprinted.

Since 1974 the IEA has helped to create a worldwide network of 100 similar institutions in over 70 countries. They are all independent but share the IEA's mission.

Views expressed in the IEA's publications are those of the authors, not those of the Institute (which has no corporate view), its Managing Trustees, Academic Advisory Council members or senior staff.

Members of the Institute's Academic Advisory Council, Honorary Fellows, Trustees and Staff are listed on the following page.

The Institute gratefully acknowledges financial support for its publications programme and other work from a generous benefaction by the late Alec and Beryl Warren.

Other papers recently published by the IEA include:

Taxation and Red Tape
The Cost to British Business of Complying with the UK Tax System
Francis Chittenden, Hilary Foster & Brian Sloan
Research Monograph 64; ISBN 978 0 255 36612 0; £12.50

Ludwig von Mises – A Primer
Eamonn Butler
Occasional Paper 143; ISBN 978 0 255 36629 8; £7.50

Does Britain Need a Financial Regulator?
Statutory Regulation, Private Regulation and Financial Markets
Terry Arthur & Philip Booth
Hobart Paper 169; ISBN 978 0 255 36593 2; £12.50

Hayek's *The Constitution of Liberty*
An Account of Its Argument
Eugene F. Miller
Occasional Paper 144; ISBN 978 0 255 36637 3; £12.50

Fair Trade Without the Froth
A Dispassionate Economic Analysis of 'Fair Trade'
Sushil Mohan
Hobart Paper 170; ISBN 978 0 255 36645 8; £10.00

A New Understanding of Poverty
Poverty Measurement and Policy Implications
Kristian Niemietz
Research Monograph 65; ISBN 978 0 255 36638 0; £12.50

The Challenge of Immigration
A Radical Solution
Gary S. Becker
Occasional Paper 145; ISBN 978 0 255 36613 7; £7.50

Sharper Axes, Lower Taxes
Big Steps to a Smaller State
Edited by Philip Booth
Hobart Paperback 38; ISBN 978 0 255 36648 9; £12.50

Other IEA publications

Comprehensive information on other publications and the wider work of the IEA can be found at www.iea.org.uk. To order any publication please see below.

Personal customers

Orders from personal customers should be directed to the IEA:
Clare Rusbridge
IEA
2 Lord North Street
FREEPOST LON10168
London SW1P 3YZ
Tel: 020 7799 8907. Fax: 020 7799 2137
Email: crusbridge@iea.org.uk

Trade customers

All orders from the book trade should be directed to the IEA's distributor:
Gazelle Book Services Ltd (IEA Orders)
FREEPOST RLYS-EAHU-YSCZ
White Cross Mills
Hightown
Lancaster LA1 4XS
Tel: 01524 68765. Fax: 01524 53232
Email: sales@gazellebooks.co.uk

IEA subscriptions

The IEA also offers a subscription service to its publications. For a single annual payment (currently £42.00 in the UK), subscribers receive every monograph the IEA publishes. For more information please contact:
Clare Rusbridge
Subscriptions
IEA
2 Lord North Street
FREEPOST LON10168
London SW1P 3YZ
Tel: 020 7799 8907. Fax: 020 7799 2137
Email: crusbridge@iea.org.uk